Planning with the Small Computer

Books from the Lincoln Institute of Land Policy/OG&H

Land Acquisition in Developing Countries
Michael G. Kitay

Introduction to Computer Assisted Valuation
Edited by Arlo Woolery and Sharon Shea

Second World Congress on Land Policy, 1983
Edited by Matthew Cullen and Sharon Woolery

The Zoning Game Revisited
Richard F. Babcock and Charles L. Siemon

Land Supply Monitoring
David R. Godschalk, Scott A. Bollens, John S. Hekman, and Mike E. Miles

Advanced Industrial Development
Donald A. Hicks

Land Markets and Land Policy in a Metropolitan Area: A Case Study of Tokyo
Yuzuru Hanayama

Land Readjustment: The Japanese System
Luciano Minerbi, Peter Nakamura, Kiyoko Nitz, and Jane Yanai

Measuring Fiscal Capacity
Edited by H. Clyde Reeves

1984 Real Estate Valuation Colloquium
A Redefinition of Real Estate Appraisal Precepts and Processes
Edited by William N. Kinnard, Jr.

The Urban Caldron
Edited by Joseph DiMento, LeRoy Graymer, and Frank Schnidman

Urban Planning for Latin America
Francis Violich, with Robert Daughters

Land Policy in Modern Indonesia
Colin MacAndrews

Economics and Tax Policy
Karl E. Case

Planning with the Small Computer

An Applications Reader

Edited by

Mathew E. MacIver
Jan Schreiber

A Lincoln Institute of Land Policy Book

Published by
Oelgeschlager, Gunn & Hain
in association with the
Lincoln Institute of Land Policy

International Standard Book Number: 0-89946-215-4

Library of Congress Catalog Card Number: 86-8462

Printed in the U.S.A.

Oelgeschlager, Gunn & Hain, Publishers, Inc.
131 Clarendon Street
Boston, MA 02116

Library of Congress Cataloging-in-Publication Data

Planning with the small computer.

"A Lincoln Institute of Land Policy book."
Includes index.
1. Local government—United States—Data processing. 2. Microcomputers. I. MacIver, Mathew. II. Schreiber, Jan, 1941– . III. Lincoln Institute of Land Policy.
JS344.E4P58 1986 352.1'028'5 86-8462
ISBN 0-88946-215-4

Contents

List of Figures and Templates

Figures

Templates

List of Tables

Lincoln Institute Foreword

The Lincoln Institute of Land Policy is an educational institute dedicated to the development and exchange of ideas and information pertaining to land policy and property taxation. It is a school offering opportunities for instruction and research. It welcomes government officials, working practitioners, and students to the pursuit of advanced studies.

The Lincoln Institute is also a center for linking the university and the practice of government; for bringing together scholars, professionals, and officials; and for blending the theory and practice of land policy. The Lincoln Institute staff are involved in many innovative and creative projects to examine the impact of emerging technology on the analysis and implementation of land and tax policy, and this volume is the result of one such effort. Mathew MacIver and Jan Schreiber have brought together in this reader a series of papers that will aid the public sector in realizing the potential efficiency of better information management and therefore better available information for public policymaking.

Planning with the Small Computer reports on the lessons learned during a phase of our computerized land management systems research effort. As our research continues, we will publish periodic reports, both in this series and in our monograph series.

Frank Schnidman
Senior Fellow
June 1986

Preface

Planning with the Small Computer is a guide to the use of microcomputer-based techniques to improve the management and use of information in local government. Most planners and other public managers understand, in general terms, that microcomputers can help them quickly organize and analyze information, but designing microcomputer-based planning applications and laying the necessary technical and political groundwork for seeing them through may be a new process for many. This volume details strategies for using this technology in local government practice and describes families of analytic procedures that are particularly well suited to a microprocessing environment.

The remarkable growth of the microcomputer industry has stemmed from the power and popularity of inexpensive generic software. These programs provide users with structural frameworks for solving a wide range of problems, regardless of data content. We have imitated that generic structure in this book. Each chapter offers general methodological approaches to different classes of planning problems. Although stock analytic responses rarely shed much light on complex problems, cases used throughout the book illustrate techniques that can be adapted to other issues. Because microcomputer-based systems let analysts rapidly test new ideas or establish new sources of information, "cookbook" solutions are, in fact, more likely to be discarded in favor of fresh, creative approaches to data management and quantitative reasoning. Choosing the best hardware configuration or software "bundle" is undoubtedly an important milestone in the system development process, but developing the "headware"—defining applications and an implementation process—is crucial to the continued success of any system. This book concentrates on principles of system and application design rather than on the ever-changing technical detail of specific pieces of hardware or software.

The first chapter establishes the links between local government organization, information needs at different levels of the organization, and appropriate types of microcomputer solutions. This is followed by a series of studies that illustrate basic data base development concepts; the use of simple descriptive and associative statistics to sense neighborhood change; principles for choosing cost-effective types of projection and forecasting methods; and the design of microcomputer-based financial impact models. Special sections are also included on geoprocessing techniques for mapping and spatial analysis, as well as the theory and structure of network analysis models. This menu is meant only to whet the appetite; extensions of these techniques become easier to imagine and create as planners build microcomputing experience.

This book is itself the culmination of an experiment. In October 1982 the Lincoln Institute of Land Policy and the city of Cleveland began a three-year collaboration to test the use of generic land management software for supporting various land policy functions in city government. John Fauquier has directly summarized some of the findings of the Cleveland project in chapter 2, but the results of our joint effort color every chapter here.

This project has enjoyed the unqualified financial and moral support of the Cleveland Foundation and the Gund Foundation, both of Cleveland, Ohio. Without their enthusiastic and sustained generosity, the project (and this book) would not have been realized. We also wish to recognize the contributions of Mayor George Voinovich of Cleveland; Hunter Morrison, director of city planning for Cleveland; Arlo Woolery, former executive director of the Lincoln Institute; and Charles Cook, former director of education and research at the Institute. Mr. Cook and one of the coeditors (J.S.) each took a turn as director of the Cleveland LMS Project. Further recognition is due John Fauquier and George Gilliam, project managers for the City of Cleveland. Finally, we must pay tribute to the many other professionals in Cleveland City Hall and in cities across the country who are building new responses to the need for better planning information in local government.

M.M.
J.S.

1

Informed Choice in Local Government: The Alternative Uses of Microcomputing Technology

Mathew E. MacIver

Since computers first appeared on the scene some thirty years ago, planners have debated their use in the profession. Initial successes with transportation modeling studies in the 1950s led in the next decade to further experimentation with more elaborate multisectoral models of urban change. Complex simulations undertaken in those years by a number of city governments yielded fewer practical benefits than originally envisioned (Brewer 1974; Lee 1973), and so in the 1960s computer-assisted methods played less of an active role in local government settings.

Within the past five years, inexpensive microcomputer hardware—and cheap, generic software—has become broadly available. The newest generation of interactive, desktop microcomputers is fully capable of supporting elaborate modeling techniques, but the versatility of the machine extends far beyond this relatively narrow niche. The advantages that microcomputers offer the planning profession bear little relation to the importance that individual planners place on the use of sophisticated analytic techniques. Regardless of stylistic bias, the substance of daily planning practice in every jurisdiction is generally very similar: zoning variance requests are studied or amended; program expenditures are tallied and compared to budget allocations; projections are prepared; and decisions are made to tax or subsidize different portions of the public weal. Microcomputers can help local governments organize the information needed to make decisions in these practical realms, using software tools to manage words, numbers, and images.

The following chapters discuss a few of these possibilities in much greater detail, but the range of potentially useful applications is virtually limitless. This is not an argument for unbridled experimentation because the costs of random system development are high. However, few managers who are now faced with decisions regarding the implementation of microcomputer-based information systems have had experience in evaluating microcomputer applications. This chapter will show how planners and other local officials can select project investments that best exploit the power of the personal computer in the context of local government choice. For convenience, the major options are discussed under three headings: (1) communication and organization, (2) monitoring, projection, and forecasting, and (3) geographic information systems.

Communication and Organization

Designing better methods to inform choice in local government begins with first viewing the microcomputer as *communication* vehicle, and only then as a tool for *computation*. This approach is useful for two reasons. First, a needs analysis based on this perspective necessarily becomes much broader because the microcomputer now appears as a link between different planning functions, rather than a self-contained data receptacle or elaborate calculator serving the needs of a single planning cadre. Therefore, more attention is placed on the connections between specific missions and operating procedures of the planning agency. Second, a communications perspective places greater weight on *information* processing rather than on *data* processing. Data are quantitative representations of fact that often have meaning only for a rather circumscribed set of users. Data become information only when they are combined and presented in a format that facilitates understanding in a broader user audience. If improved communication becomes the primary goal in designing a planning information system, individual analysts will be forced to judge the quality of their internal data handling procedures according to whether or not they communicate useful information. In other words, methods used to evaluate the usefulness of data will be applied in a more extroverted fashion.

For this reason, decision makers need to examine the organizational impacts of microcomputer technology before developing new kinds of applications. There are sure to be differences in interpretations of what is or is not the right information for the right client, and most organizational models break down when they are applied to ever more specific situations. But starting with a limited, insular model of the executive functions of local government provides new system managers with a primitive structure on which they can build a more realistic set of analytic expectations. The model used here consists of three governmental layers, distinguished by their basic functional responsibilities, the characteristics of decisions they are likely to take, and the information needed to inform those decisions.

The Operations Level

The goal of the first, or *operations,* level is to ensure that the day-to-day government services are being provided to the community. These services are guided by internal administrative procedures designed to support policy mandates from the executive, the appropriate legislative body, or, in special cases, the judiciary. Work at this level is oriented to the direct delivery of community goods and services (such as road maintenance, police and fire protection, trash collection, and the like). If it is true, as Woody Allen once opined, that "eighty percent of success is showing up," then the overriding objective here is to make sure that resources are showing up when and where they are supposed to. These resources support direct, measurable actions that provide clear benefits to small subsets of a community.

The choices governing action in this layer are incremental, repetitive, small (individually) in scope, and bounded closely by a limited set of alternative responses. They are also inward looking; achievement is measured primarily against definitions of performance internal to the layer rather than externally defined community goals. Exceptions that prove the concept could be cited from operational units given more autonomous control, such as police precinct commanders who are at some liberty to redirect staff and materiel temporarily to cover unexpected situations. Still, more rigid and formalized chains of command in police work act as a counterweight to fully discretionary action.

Operational information must be collected, processed, and distributed to serve these needs. Information is not useful unless it is suitably specific ("How big is their proposed setback?"); constantly updated ("Do we need to put three people or four people on this job today?"); and in some cases, more or less available in real time ("The alarm came in *two hours* ago?"). Processing such information is a matter of keeping lists of things and events, rather than changing data into synthesized information for the enlightenment of others. Close coordination is sometimes necessary for collecting and disseminating data between operational entities, but this is often very difficult because of the precision required of data at this level. Data elements are often defined so that they are only useful for one very specific function.

The Policy Level

By contrast, activities at the other end of the organizational spectrum are a little more free wheeling. Elected government officials interpret public attitudes to secure support for decisions regarding the gross allocation of public resources. The result is policy: strategic heuristics that may be codified through political statements, executive orders, legislative initiatives, and budgetary recommendations. Policy is set to formalize government priorities, to stabilize political consensus (even only momentarily), and finally, to guide and evaluate tactical government actions. Making policy is a matter not of unilaterally concocting rules but rather of systematically codifying decisions to support different combinations of specific development goals. These include any actions needed to persuade other policy makers of the wisdom of any combination of decisions. The necessity of policy tradeoffs and the difficulties in altering existing regulatory or budgetary parameters often severely limit the power of policy makers to effect change.

Because of the complexity and the ramifications of decision making at this macro level, techniques for modeling the effects of decisions can be very useful. Scenarios constructed to summarize the consequences of alternative action are likely to be unique from case to case, each featuring a complex variety of possible impacts on different constituencies. Tradeoffs must often be chosen on the basis of incomplete information, most of which is numerically incomparable across issues.

Both anecdotal and numerical information is used to inform decisions at policy levels, and descriptive information of either type must be summarized to facilitate analysis. Daily editorials, for instance, are often condensed to compare shades of popular opinion with political decisions, taken or contemplated. But the information is more useful if a one-page memorandum, delivered as the papers hit the street, is used to do the job. The quality of numerical information at policy levels is determined in a similar way. Accurate, timely quantitative information is essential, but only if it can be aggregated quickly and cross-checked against multiple sources. Graphic presentation formats, such as charts and graphs, also make it easier to understand aggregated information. But summary numerical data are not stand-alone products in the same way as daily newspaper excerpts are. Aggregated information is used most often only as a foundation to search for exceptions, anomalies, and trends that run counter to expectations. There is also one other important difference between anecdotal and numerical indicators: measurement biases and the limits of inferential reasoning are not writ as boldly as headlines are, but even among laymen scientific sophistication is increasing, and virtually every politician will dismiss as specious the results of any statistical operation that is inadequately explained or purports to produce definitive evidence of causality.

The Management Level

The management level is the bridge between operations and policy, and it is here that most planners, managers, and policy analysts will ply their trade. Public managers design ways to sense community change, describe the effects of existing government interventions, and evaluate the probable consequences of different government actions. This covers a lot of bases, and so we might find it easier to split this general definition into a few specific responsibilities.

First, public managers supervise line operations in specialized departments, making sure that services are delivered according to internal performance goals. Traditional planning functions would certainly fall under this heading, most notably the administration of zoning and subdivision regulations. But in recent times planners have joined the ranks of other public managers by specializing in the administration of similar line functions, such as public works, social service administration, and economic development programing. If goals are not met, departmental operating procedures or existing combinations of intradepartmental resources may have to be changed.

Second, managers evaluate the delivery of services according to their impact on the community, collecting and analyzing data to correlate levels of public service with measurements of public benefit. Studies of this sort may lead to broader redefinitions of internal operating responsibilities across many different departments.

Finally, a manager may also be called on to search for longer-term patterns and trends that will affect the composition of more fundamental policy guidelines. Baseline studies undertaken for comprehensive planning purposes are classic examples of this type of projection and forecasting exercise. Although the impact of comprehensive planning recommendations may not become clear for several years, all such recommendations contain assumptions concerning projected and prescribed distributions of public resources.

These jobs are united in a single common purpose: to provide a means for exercising balanced, comparative judgment in the allocation of government resources, even though the options for acting on that judgment may not rest in the hands of the manager. "The test of a first rate intelligence," said F. Scott Fitzgerald, "is the ability to hold two opposed ideas in mind at the same time and still retain the ability to function." The public manager's job is to build analytic crucibles to hold and shape conflicting sets of ideas so that government can respond to change.

Some managers, particularly in line departments, may make the occasional decision that directly affects the delivery of community goods and services, or the internal organization of government operations. Most of the manager's discretionary influence, however, is exercised in deciding how to *measure* internal and external government performance and how to *distribute* this information up and down the organizational ladder. Planners design and use measurement schemes to better understand the causes of community change and, equally important, to communicate their views of change to those who wield political power. Measurement issues are numerous, and weighing the tradeoffs involved in the use of one or another analytic technique may be only a minor part of the problem.

One basic question is whether or not a responsible use of numerical information is possible in the first place. Skilled analysts, quality data, or receptive clients may be missing or in short supply, thus pushing the analyst toward the use of carefully reasoned anecdotal "hunches." If the requisites exist and there is a clear advantage to developing solutions based on quantitative reasoning, then limits must be placed on the amount of time and money spent on reaching conclusions—even if the conclusions are incomplete or contradictory. Uncertainty can never be completely removed from any decision, and so fail-safe points must be built into an analytic project to ensure periodic self-assessment before mandatory external assessment is needed to refocus work. By contrast, there is usually no difficulty in terminating analysis that is undeniably leading to conclusions that are moot or unacceptable to political leadership.

Distributing information also goes beyond a simple concern for making sure that quantitative conclusions are presented in easily comprehensible forms. How much emphasis, for instance, should be placed on preparing systems for monitoring routine information needs and how much should be placed on building up the flexibility needed to repeatedly respond to ad hoc data requests? Are there ways to combine procedures for data collection and distribution that can help improve the overall flow of information between each layer of the organizational pyramid? Finally, how can managers know when information is being used more effectively?

These questions are usually asked in relation to particular planning or management problems, rather than as umbrella generalizations to redirect the way that whole organizations operate. Information used to inform these decisions is usually gathered and applied in the same way, on the basis of individual talents, time, data availability, smaller-scale organizational opportunities or constraints, and the like. When problems are discovered, analysts usually think anecdotally about choosing the tools that have been used with success in similar situations in the past. Because the microcomputer has not until recently figured prominently in the options that managers can consider, "muddling through" in this manner has worked pretty well. Managers in government are discovering, however, that theirs is the occupational niche that will be most profoundly affected by microcomputer technology and that their analytic and communicative options are widening considerably. Managers are discovering, in fact, that they will bear the primary responsibility for the effective use of microcomputer technology throughout the entire organization. Why should the primary responsibility for system development and implementation fall to management end users, who usually lack formalized computer training? What about the ubiquitous system professionals who, over the years, have coordinated the use of larger computers with the softer functions of government? One answer is that the overall growth of the industry will place many more micros on the desks of managers than can be adequately supported by a relatively smaller number of data processing professionals. This does not treat the entire issue, however.

A more useful answer is that large machines spawned, in their own right, an organizational structure oriented to the most efficient use of a highly complex, costly resource. In order to optimize the allocation of computer services, organizations had to adapt to the needs of the machine, changing the ways that information was collected and disseminated through a single, centralized source. The microcomputer, on the other hand, is a tool whose efficiency increases in rough proportion to the degree of *de*centralization available in organizations, which will now cause information technologies to adapt much more quickly and explicitly to finer shades of organizational mandate. This is an oversimplification, as is the organizational model used above; data processing personnel certainly can be extremely helpful in isolating important technical trends and pitfalls. But managers have to take the initiative, since they are the ones who have the most accurate understanding of the adaptability that must be built into information systems to serve each layer of government administration. Microcomputers can answer the call for flexibility, but managers must learn how and when a microcomputer-based system can best be put to use on a daily basis. To examine the applications is to review the classic functions of the planning office.

Monitoring, Projection, and Forecasting

There is undoubtedly a risk in using another somewhat Procrustean model to describe the seemingly disjointed, intuitive, and predominantly informal application of method that characterizes the typical urban planner. He (or she) daily confronts problems that Norman Steissel, the New York City sanitation commissioner, once described as "organized and focused chaos." But if we erect modest methodological schemata alongside our model of organizational structure, each will act as a foil for the other to illustrate basic system planning guidelines and to highlight the important singularities that managers must be aware of to avoid turning an extra length of flexibility into a very tight noose.

Monitoring Systems

Monitoring is a fundamental function of any microcomputer-based planning and management system. However, as was evident in our discussion of governmental information needs, this activity means different things to different people. For line departments, monitoring systems track building permits, schedule inspections, trace infrastructure maintenance activities, or keep records on human service clients. Monitoring in this environment means capturing, updating, and selectively distributing highly detailed information for narrowly defined purposes. The system development emphasis at this level is therefore placed on designing computer record formats and procedures for sorting and selecting subsets of data stored in these formats. The purposes of these systems are similar in that they are all used to describe and direct very specific things or actions. They are also united in the dissimilarity of their data content.

A premium is placed at this level on specific detail and accuracy, and so record formats and updating procedures are very strictly controlled. They are also most efficiently administered in a centralized fashion. The adaptability of these data bases to functions other than those for which they were originally designed is generally limited, at least without substantial modification. Yet much specialized information can be useful to other departments at the same level or to managers concerned with community trends or changes in government performance. For instance, portions of the data collected for a building inspection monitoring system could be extremely useful to fire departments, just as summary information concerning zoning variance applications could be useful to planners examining shifts in community land use patterns. In the former example, line departments could profit from a horizontal exchange of information. In the latter example, a vertical transfer of information could be effected using simple aggregational techniques.

Facilitating the exchange of data, then, becomes a major goal in designing a cost-effective monitoring system. One obvious option would be to remove all data redundancies between different systems and construct more highly centralized data processing facilities to serve the needs of all operational departments dealing with similar substantive areas. The increasing availability of less expensive, multi-user systems, including those based on the microcomputer, certainly makes this a more attractive possibility, but often ignored are the fundamental differences between the data needed by different government entities. Data differ according to scale of measurement, periodicity (the time data remain useful before updating), frequency of use, required access time, and a host of other characteristics. The goal of reducing redundancy may be elusive if it becomes impossible to strike compromises between departments with slightly but significantly different data requirements. Turf issues also complicate the picture.

A better way of approaching this problem might be to seek an *optimum* data redundancy, using data exchange procedures that are not dependent on the way each department stores its data. Most microcomputer software packages have the ability to convert their data into characters that can be read by other machines or software packages, and more software is appearing now that can subdivide and selectively import or export small pieces of differently structured files. Sometimes it can even be more cost effective to have a clerk key enter updates into a hybrid file using selected source files originating in other departments. In this way, different sources of information can be integrated without harming the integrity of the individual files, and integration can occur at a pace that is not dictated by the slowest member of the coalition. Chapter 2 addresses these issues in some detail, and in a paper published elsewhere I have offered a specific calculus that can be used to compare different kinds of data transfer options (MacIver 1984).

Monitoring at management and policy levels is less concerned with tracking specific incidents or conditions than it is with discovering broader patterns of community change based on summary information. Most microcomputer data base management systems include utilities to select, sort, and extract useful indicators of change from operational departments. Planning departments rarely use these utilities, since, by informal tradition, planners have regarded themselves as data users and not data collectors. However, data collection and exchange techniques can wean planners away from an unreasonably strong dependence on census data (which is always out of date) in favor of fresher, better targeted intelligence gathered from existing sources. These include operational departments as well as nontraditional sources such as local realtors, insurance companies, utility companies, and other data-intensive businesses. The key in both data collection strategies is to establish an effective quid pro quo that will repay—with processed, aggregated information or some other useful government product—a consistently measured and collected source of data. The use of microcomputer-based data management packages may also reduce overhead processing costs to the point where funds can be justified to conduct specialized sample surveys pinpointing subtle demographic shifts or changes in local economic conditions.

To summarize, monitoring gives us snapshots that describe events and conditions with accuracy and timeliness appropriate to each layer of executive responsibility. Monitoring also provides a necessary foundation for discovering important relationships between events and conditions that, if interpreted correctly, give governments the ability to intervene constructively in the process of urban development.

Projection and Forecasting

Tornadoes, tidal waves, and earthquakes number among the few powerful forces of change that act in perfect random isolation from other factors to alter the shape and character of human settlements. Other less dramatic agents of change work in concert and over greater periods of time, with sometimes equally traumatic results. *Projection* techniques are used to improve our understanding of the connections among trends in land use, housing conditions, the economy, movement patterns, and other sectoral divisions that we concoct to measure the quality of urban life. They allow us to make and test inferences from these trends. Projections are tools we use to extend past performance into the future, using assumptions concerning conditions that we know existed at the time at which change occurred. *Forecasts,* by contrast, are projections (sometimes several in combination) coupled with the explicit or implicit statement, "This is what the future will (probably) be like." A forecast is often based on conditions we believe will exist at the times for which it is constructed.

We might use the view from the rearview mirror of an automobile to *project* how the car will behave as it continues to move forward. If we actually used the rearview mirror alone while driving the car forward, we would be *forecasting* under the assumptions that, first, the car would behave the same way as it did up to this point and, second, the clear roadway we see behind us will not lead us over a cliff. This analogy is not quite perfect in that it underestimates the risks attached to using forecasts in local government. If we could be assured that the effects of government interventions were as cleanly predictable as even the least reliable of automobiles, then we would only have to worry about assumptions concerning the condition of the road ahead.

This cautionary comparison is not intended to show that projection and forecasting are worthless; they are in fact the only tools we have for envisioning the future. But the need for extreme care in scrutinizing assumptions should be obvious. Projections and forecasts are more likely to be used on a regular basis by management and policy staff than by operations staff. Managers, in particular, must make explicit decisions concerning levels of investment for the purposes of projection and prediction. Different methods require different types of data, some of which may be more or less costly or accurate than others. Methods differ tremendously in complexity, some placing extravagant demands on the quantitative expertise usually available at local levels. It is important to bear in mind that elected or appointed policy officials work under severe time constraints, in two senses. They must, of course, meet severe deadlines in many instances. But beyond this, the amount of attention they can devote to any one issue at any one time is extremely limited, arguing in favor of techniques that are easily explained and yield possibly less accurate but more explicit results. Simple techniques, consistently applied, are therefore more likely to satisfy the conditions of extreme urgency and competition for attention that often accompany policy disputes. (Parenthetically, these conditions also encourage the establishment of ongoing monitoring systems, using indicators that can be tapped on very short notice to supply useful material for speculative analysis.)

Advocating the use of simple, inexpensive, and quickly implemented techniques is not the same as advocating the use of inferior analysis to present unsupported advice. Analysis is inferior if it has been applied incorrectly, or if the analyst attributes greater authority to forecasts than the data and the precision of measurement warrant. It is harder to stretch the applicability of results derived from simple models than to make elaborate, but ultimately more tenuously contrived, system simulations appear authoritative in complex cases. William Alonso, a noted planner and scholar, has shown that severe error propagation can readily occur in complex modeling constructions that chain together combinations of arithmetic functions. Complex models can be extremely useful for fundamental research purposes, but they are best elaborated in the university, where intellectual risk can be encouraged in isolation from direct action or the contingencies of political choice. To use Alonso's terminology, "short, blunt" models of urban change present many advantages to analysts who directly support government decision making (Alonso 1968).

There are many useful families of techniques that satisfy such functional decision constraints and can be implemented using generic software operating on stand-alone microcomputer systems. Simple descriptive statistics using standard measures of centrality or dispersion can be useful for comparative work in two dimensions—over time and distance. Measures of association, constructed using two-way frequency distributions, can also be used with great advantage to discover significant exceptions to expected conditions. Population projections, economic base studies, one-off bivariate regression models, and more tactical project evaluation studies using discounted cash flow methods can all be supported using spreadsheet software. Later chapters describe each of these families of techniques, all of which can be supported with easily obtainable and understandable software.

The creative use of projection and forecasting techniques is certainly not limited to data collected at management and policy levels. If efficient data exchange procedures have been worked out, the detailed impacts of more general policy decisions can be tested quickly using data collected for administrative purposes. One example is the use of data base selection and sorting capabilities to anticipate the impacts, in some detail, of more generally framed zoning policy decisions. Some jurisdictions, for instance, may need to consider so-called sliver ordinances to impose height restrictions on very deep lots with disproportionately smaller street frontages. The idea, of course, is to minimize building shadow. But which sections of the city will be most profoundly affected by the ordinance? Is there any one group of owners that may present a legal challenge to the ruling? How big a job will it be to update the maps? Given that a city has available a file of information on vacant parcels that includes an address, owner's name, and basic dimensional information, all of these questions can be answered using virtually any standard microcomputer data base management package. More sophisticated network analysis routines can similarly be used to trace the operational traffic impacts that would occur as a result of alternative development patterns, parking schemes, or road improvement programs. Chapter 7 describes the fundamentals of network analysis. It is supported, again, by several currently available software products.

Geographic Information Systems

Nearly all information systems used in local government are geographic information systems (GIS), in one sense or another, since almost every operational or policy decision has locational ramifications and is supported by location-based data. I use the phrase here, however, to refer to computer software that can store maps in digital form for subsequent use in connection with numerical information. Such software can graphically display either the location of specific, physical elements of the urban landscape or the distribution of geographically referenced socioeconomic characteristics. In other words, a mapping system is not just a system that draws pictures but one that can directly reference and display numerical information (or attribute information) that is linked to the different map elements. Maps are tools that can summarize the locational consequences of decisions with striking effect.

Like other data bases, maps are used for different purposes at different levels of local government. There is certainly more of a need for geographical precision when it comes to pinpointing the exact location of a water main or a fire call box. Those personnel who have a greater interest in making sure that the backhoe operator digs in the right spot will place a greater premium on accuracy. Public safety workers may also place additional value on locational information that can be quickly retrieved. The types of GIS that best serve these purposes are those that can store large quantities of precise locational data yet need not store a great deal of attribute information for each of the elements that are mapped. There is a tradeoff here, particularly with the microcomputer-based systems now emerging to fill these requirements. Systems that can store large quantities of map information usually have little if any room remaining to store data that describe these elements or to accommodate the statistical analysis routines that can summarize or process attribute information. Systems designed to store and manipulate large, locationally precise data sets are usually based on mini- or mainframe computer systems that find sufficient use at operational levels without needing to tackle other jobs requiring the aggregation of socioeconomic information.

But these are the types of jobs that are most in demand at management and policy levels. It is important at this level to describe graphically the distributive consequences of public policy. Great accuracy and resolution are not needed in these types of applications; instead, strong links to attribute data as well as to the tools of statistical analysis are required. Programs that perform these functions must be designed to simplify the process of geographic data entry and editing in order to respond more quickly and with less locational detail to the needs of managers and policy staff with little if any prior computer training. Flexibility is also needed to shift gears quickly to display different kinds of thematic maps.

Geographic information systems can make it possible to use more esoteric centrographic analysis techniques, roughly the two-dimensional equivalent of the descriptive and inferential statistical operations that are currently used in research work (Norcliffe 1977). Because the potential benefit of these more specialized tools is open to the same type of questioning as are sophisticated inferential models of urban change, it is not likely that they will see widespread government use in the immediate future. In the meantime, GIS techniques can be used to great effect for monitoring, projection, and forecasting, given careful attention to the benefits and costs tied to each family of the technology.

The sequence of strategies presented in this chapter is echoed, not coincidentally, by the progression of detailed examples offered in the following chapters. These illustrations can be successfully adapted for local use, but they should not be used to the exclusion of other similarly creative information management projects designed to respond more directly to the different circumstances of each jurisdiction. Regardless of the source of a technique, however, planners should keep in mind that successful projects always initially derive from a careful examination of organizational needs. Without such an examination, our growing ability to shape technology—instead of reshaping ourselves to serve technology—would be wasted.

References

Alonso, William. 1968. "Predicting Best with Imperfect Data." *Journal of the American Institute of Planners* 34:248–255.

Brewer, Gary D. 1974. *Politicians, Bureaucrats, and the Consultant.* New York: Basic Books.

Catanese, Anthony James. 1979. "Information for Planning." In *The Practice of Local Government Planning,* edited by Frank So. Washington, D.C.: International City Management Association.

Hirschman, Albert O. 1967. *Development Projects Observed.* Washington, D.C.: The Brookings Institution.

Lee, Douglass B., Jr. 1973. "Requiem for Large Scale Models." *Journal of the American Institute of Planners* 39:163–178.

MacIver, Mathew E. 1984. "Data Sharing Methods for Land Records Systems." In *The Changing Role of Computers in Public Agencies,* edited by Rolf Schmitt. Washington, D.C.: Urban and Regional Information Systems Association.

Norcliffe, G.B., ed. 1977. *Inferential Statistics for Geographers: An Introduction.* London: Hutchinson.

Peters, Thomas J., and Robert H. Waterman, Jr. 1982. *In Search of Excellence.* New York: Harper & Row.

Slater, David C. 1984. *The Management of Local Government Planning.* Washington, D.C.: International City Management Association.

2

Taking Stock: Data Base Development Techniques

John E. Fauquier

What are the alternatives to data bases? Sometimes it seems as if they are recent inventions, a fashionable product of the computer age. However, if a data base is considered to be merely the orderly collection of information, then data bases in planning have existed at least since the beginning of the profession's modern period, which dates back to the 1860s. Those early data bases (and many contemporary ones as well) were constructed of plat maps, paper files, zoning maps, policy papers, and reports. Such collections of planning paraphernalia may not appear to be data bases because the output never appears on a neatly printed page, but they do contain all the fundamental characteristics of qualitative and quantitative data arranged in systematic ways. The old systems lacked the modern ability to categorize and manipulate data at high speeds and with great accuracy only because everything was manual. Also, the separate planning projects could not be joined together into a linked network. But these drawbacks should not obscure the fact that the work represented the operation of a planning system. Parcels were being numbered, indexed, and recorded; reports were being written that summarized gathered data; and maps portrayed spatial relationships much as they do now. Analysis and professional judgment were then used (as one hopes they still are today) to summarize masses of data. We can conclude that it is not so much the kinds of information that have changed as the ways in which we use information and the expectations we have fostered in ourselves regarding its power and predictive capabilities.

Are there vehicles other than data bases that can provide the same service? With respect to information systems, we can work only with either a data base structure (however loosely defined and poorly implemented) or, in its absence, a random collection of data. Only data bases can provide the structure necessary for efficient and effective information dissemination.

Are there situations in which data bases should not be developed? Perhaps some jurisdictions are too small to justify the implementation of a data base system; even so, reasonably priced microcomputers allow even the smallest office to use inexpensive preprogrammed software packages. The use of data bases is not inherently good or bad—only appropriate or inappropriate to a specific application. This chapter is concerned with the effective matching of carefully considered situational needs to the best data base structure available.

The following discussion will develop general principles of data base design but will also draw on the direct experience of the city of Cleveland's development departments (Economic Development, Community Development, and the City Planning Commission). The general principles are based on a theoretical discussion, simplified to extract general conclusions and observations. In order to integrate practical material, Cleveland will be used as a case study on the basis of its recent extensive experience in setting up a data base system. I was closely involved in the project throughout its life span. Even though many of the Cleveland data base projects are still in their formative stages, interesting lessons can be learned here. The reader should note that the Cleveland experience emphasizes microcomputers rather than minicomputers or mainframes and is concerned more with land management systems than alternative data bases such as project management systems. Nevertheless, many of the points made here can be generalized.

The Basic Problem

Data bases are difficult to design and implement in government or public sector agencies because in a large, complex, and ever-shifting environment they combine the science of information systems, the art of planning (land management, urban design, zoning, social planning, or transportation planning), and the art of management as expressed through the political process. This confusing blend of art and science presents formidable challenges because the systems with which we are concerned are too large to allow us to collect all relevant data and are too complex to be modeled realistically. Figure 2.1 shows schematically how this multifaceted problem can be divided into four components. The two largest components have physical properties and manifestations, and the two smallest are intangible. Systems decisions concern:

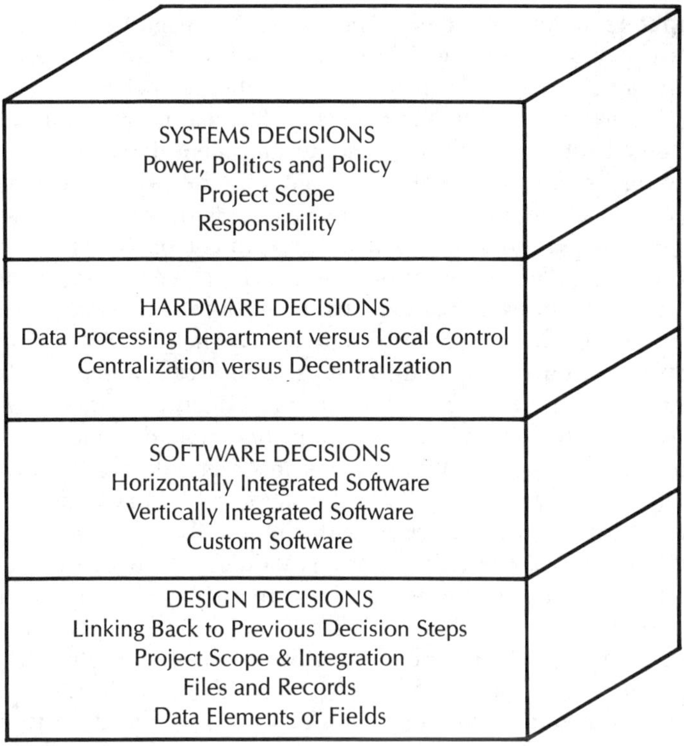

Figure 2.1. *Decision set for data base design.*

Broad policy issues

Hardware issues or physical equipment needs

Software decisions, including the ways data are catalogued and processed

Design decisions that determine the interrelationships among data elements, records, fields, and files.

A description of each decision type and the supporting issues follows, using Cleveland city departments as an example.

The Cleveland Land Management System (LMS)

In October 1982 the Lincoln Institute of Land Policy and the city of Cleveland agreed to a three-year joint project that would employ microcomputers in developing new approaches to the gathering, processing, and dissemination of land-related data. Software, training, and consultation were provided by the Institute, whereas personnel and policy approval were contributed by City Hall. The main activity for the project was to be centered in the so-called development departments, with the Planning Commission as the lead agency. The project developers believed that at the end of the three-year period, the systems would be completely operational and that city personnel familiar with them would continue to find new applications and uses for this emerging technology.

The SOLIR software package, the heart of the new system, is a menu-driven collection of modules developed by the Lincoln Institute. The modules fall into three main groups. The first is a generic data base management package that allows users to structure data elements and records flexibly to create a diverse range of various data files. In addition, there are two other families of programs that enhance SOLIR's utility as a land management tool: (1) the statistical and analytical modules, which are used in conjunction with the data base (often for property valuation), and (2) the geoprocessing modules, which are used to digitize and store spatial coordinates as well as to display several types of user-specified maps, where features can vary according to data contained in the data base. All three functions are linked together so that a full range of data manipulation and analysis is possible.

The Cleveland LMS project was designed to introduce the SOLIR software to senior and middle management of the city and to identify projects that could benefit almost immediately from the available tools. Most of the initial efforts were used to identify good candidate projects and to define and devise data structures; these first phases of the project took a good deal of time on the part of both city and Institute staff. As staff gained experience, the pace of the project quickened considerably, since using the systems takes less of a focused, concerned effort than developing them initially.

Some of the first projects were designed to systematize records of vacant lands. These were appropriate initial ventures because they were inventories of data with relatively simple structures and because the applications had basic statistical needs and no requirements for mapping techniques. Such relatively uncomplicated applications provided an opportunity to get started on projects that, first, had low "investment" costs (data largely assembled and structured) and, second, could be easily abandoned if unsuccessful. We soon discovered that one of the major benefits of the microcomputer-based system is that novel project ideas can be tried out quickly and cheaply, without the heavy investment of time, money, and programming resources more typical of mainframe environments. This type of basic project has interesting growth potential; future developments could integrate mapping capabilities and statistical analysis.

Subsequent projects had similar parcel-based data file types. One of particular interest was the Historic Inventory, a complete listing of all the historic buildings and districts in the city of Cleveland. Another was the Arson Early Warning System, developed in conjunction with a neighborhood group concerned with high local levels of arson. Although the data base was only a prototype test of concept for a larger system established outside the city, the smaller system could, through appropriate statistical techniques, identify properties with a profile that experience had shown to be especially vulnerable to arson. Another of the larger projects undertaken in the early stages was called the Target Area Investment Program. It was designed to obtain a complete picture of both physical and social attributes of a depressed core area of the city.

Recent work has focused on more elaborate projects with sophisticated statistical and mapping needs. The Land Bank program is a real-time data base that was developed to track all parcels that accrued to the city through tax foreclosure or other means. Because of constant buying and selling activity as well as court decisions affecting these parcels, it is necessary to have accurate and current information. A future development of this program might include a mapping project to identify and digitize parcels so that their distribution throughout the city can be more easily analyzed.

A data base on city-owned property is currently being developed to track and monitor all of the properties that the city owns. It may later be linked with the Land Bank program for better coordination and to yield a more complete picture of the land market for policy and assessment purposes. Yet another advanced project is a commercial strip monitoring task. The succession of land uses is being catalogued and analyzed, using, again, the mapping component of the software to identify land use patterns over time and across the city.

In the final stages of the Land Management System project, manuals were written to document applications techniques that have been developed and to provide a consistent and high-quality set of reference tools. These will allow faster and better training of professional planning personnel by documenting systems procedures already in place and by leading new planners through the steps of constructing data bases, entering data, making maps, and performing various types of analysis.

The next four sections discuss the major decision levels identified in Figure 2.1. If we view the whole matter of getting a data base designed and implemented as a system, then we can apply systems principles to the task to obtain a preliminary view that obscures real details and exceptions but provides a simplified set of patterns (a model) that clearly describes the major themes.

The Systems Decisions

The global overview, or the big picture, represents the highest levels of the administration that approve the prerequisite projects and budgets. Here also the most complex policy interactions take place. The three topics embraced by this global overview are (1) the interaction of power, politics, and policy as they affect the design and implementation of data bases; (2) the resources available for carrying out the project, and (3) responsibility, or who is in charge of the project. Each of these is discussed by presenting both the theoretical material that establishes a set of reference points and also the practical issues as they were confronted in Cleveland.

Power, Politics, and Policy

Government and public sector agencies work within a set of constraints and boundaries. These are determined and defined by the interaction patterns of all the people and institutions that deal with a set of issues. In the case of planning, many service departments interact, including engineering, law, community development, economic development, social planning, zoning, and urban design. There is also an important set of interactions with political offices. Planning departments are preoccupied with land—how it is classified, used, stored, disposed of, rehabilitated, sold, leveled, bermed, and modified—and agreement on how land *should* be treated is forever under debate. Therefore, information systems are needed to provide the most accurate data for management decision making, and to help build a partnership between the politician and the professional planner.

In their largest aspects, political decisions have little or nothing to do with the technical aspects of systems or data bases. Their main focus is on politics and money, power and control. Therefore, before any technical decisions are made, the manager must have a thorough understanding of these other processes and how they affect the specific environment being addressed. *Locus of control* is a term applied to the general amount of power that a manager has at his disposal. Well beyond power, however, are the associated ways that data gets collected, used, analyzed, and transformed. The higher up the organizational ladder one goes, the wider the locus of control.

The first order of business, therefore, is to establish the right climate for development. This means that approval for the development of a new system must be cleared through to the highest levels of the organization. It is unwise to try to develop a system first and then gain approval afterward, since the resulting psychological setting is likely to be one of wariness and caution if not outright resistance. At this stage, top-down system planning is required. Bottom-up planning is appropriate for other parts of the systems task, particularly to ensure a well-integrated project.

As Mathew MacIver noted in chapter 1, three distinct management levels exist in any planning environment, and we will consider them as distinct and typical of most management environments. For our purposes we will relabel them slightly, and call them the policy level, the department level, and the operational level. Figure 2.2 shows a simple conceptual diagram of the three levels. Let us examine some of their information characteristics in relation to data properties, projects, reporting, and geoprocessing.

At the top level, the major policy decisions are made by senior politicians and senior civil servants. The decision to create a data base is never taken in isolation, and the decision makers at this level will feel obliged to place such a decision within a very broad context. (In fact, the idea of creating a data base rarely occurs here first. It is usually the result of a need felt at the departmental level.) Many typical concerns involve political impact. For instance, a mayor might ask what consequences would be paid by a city if planning were not modernized with computer-based monitoring and analysis systems. Alternatively, the question might be turned around and asked in a way that would require the expense and creation of a new data base to justify its own existence. (Some modern approaches have used cost/benefit analysis for such issues.) The would-be system manager must have this initial situation carefully analyzed to determine the likelihood of obtaining approval for the project. If the political scene does not favor the choice to computerize a data base, what does the manager do? There are really only two possible responses. First, one might discard the attempt to seek

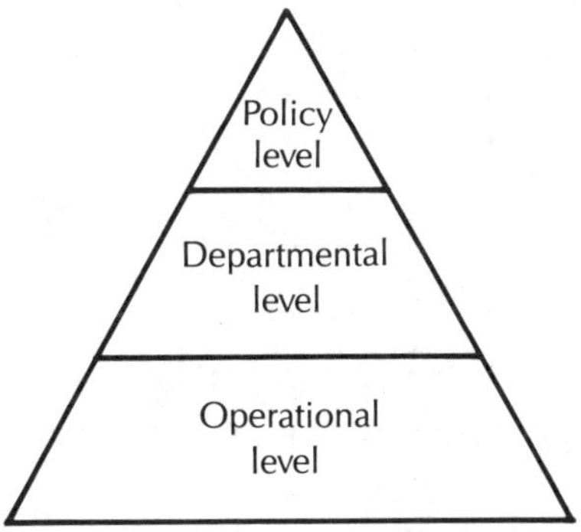

Figure 2.2. *Management hierarchy.*

approval for a computerized data base and go back to the manual methods currently in use (*somebody* considers present methods adequate to do the job). On the other hand, there is always the option of lobbying to change negative attitudes. Many political figures have no particular liking for electronic data processing techniques and have a stubborn bias against such projects. If the manager feels that a newly designed data base is vital to the operation of the agency, then the project must be sold to the people who are responsible for the decision at the highest level.

The departmental level is the critical middle that must communicate with the policy level and the day-to-day functioning of the operational level. This is the area from which the primary thrust for data base systems often comes. It is then necessary to sell the plan to the policy makers above and to convince the line staff below that the job can be done well.

The operational level is occupied by line personnel involved in planning, computer programming, systems analysis, data gathering, and data entry. It is here where the small details get put together into a working system. The policy level gives approval and then delegates the task of implementing the system. The departmental level gives some general directives and goals to achieve, but it is at the operational level that the daily work gets done.

Cleveland's mayor George Voinovich was in favor of instituting the Land Management System project and provided approval from the top at the outset. However, some of the middle-level managers were not experienced with such novel planning techniques and required some convincing. It is important to note that the approval of middle-level managers is just as important as approval at senior levels because after the initial sign-off, senior management is rarely involved in projects on a day-to-day basis; a project is doomed if it does not have the confidence of middle-level staff. Ultimately, motivated staff from various departments were assigned to the project, bringing to it a variety of backgrounds and skills. Instruction was provided to acquaint all operational staff with the needs of the project and the principles of data base theory and practice.

The Scope of the Project

Three vital components of every data base project must be defined and assessed at this stage: project funding levels and sources; the personnel who will perform programing, application development, and user-support work; and the length of time the project will take to design, implement, and evaluate. In their enthusiasm to implement new projects, project advocates sometimes forget about the practical limits determined by these three important items. A careful needs assessment, well documented and presented, can often determine success or failure in getting approval for a data base project.

In Cleveland the LMS project was created as a consortium of government, research agency (Lincoln Institute of Land Policy), and public foundations (the Cleveland Foundation and Gund Foundation, who cosponsored it). Each of these groups had basic interests to satisfy. The city, heavy with staff but light on budget, was nonetheless able to participate, given support from the other parties. The Lincoln Institute was able to test new SOLIR software. And the foundations were able to fund a project that had legitimate and definable public interest goals. The scope of the project was well defined and monitored by drafting a formal proposal that had to be approved for each of the three years of the project.

Responsibilities

After a project is approved, responsibility lies with the highest member of the decision-making team that approved the project. Therefore, an important caution is in order: the manager must not promise products that cannot be delivered. The political process is notoriously merciless when confronted with empty promises.

In very large planning projects, responsibility does not always rest in the hands of only one person. While good management practice dictates that one individual have final responsibility, the authority to make important commitments is, in fact, divided among several people with different skills or interests: one person could be responsible for the planning and design phase of the project, a second for the implementation and testing phase, and a third for the operational and monitoring phase.

The responsibility in the Cleveland project rested mainly with the project director from the Lincoln Institute of Land Policy because the project was initially proposed by the Institute, which also provided much of the funding, assigned many of the resources, and proposed the schedule of events for each of the three project years. The city of Cleveland also appointed a project manager to coordinate the selection of subprojects to be included in the larger effort as well as to maintain links among project staff. Each of these managers had an important role to play in the ongoing development of the project.

In summary, the large-scale decisions made at the outset of any data base design project have the broadest, most general impact. Projects proposed at high management levels tend to be planned "top-down," and those that arise from the grass roots are usually termed examples of "bottom-up" planning. No one technique or style is better than the other, and the best systems show evidence of design work having occurred concurrently (and cooperatively) at several levels.

Hardware Decisions

Decision making in the hardware portion of the data base design exercise affects part of the physical system: staff must determine (1) whether the data base should be managed and operated by the data processing department or rather placed under local control and (2) whether systems will be more or less centralized.

Data Processing Department Versus Local Control

Data processing departments had extensive control of computers and computer resources when mainframes were the only machines available. The advent of the microcomputer has shifted the locus of control down the management hierarchy and onto desktops in individual offices. However, despite the inroads made by microcomputers, most jurisdictions still require some services from their data processing departments. Even so, the proliferation of commercially available software has led many managers to exercise total control over their own data base systems. The decision on which route to follow must be made carefully. Each available computing resource must be evaluated, and, of equal importance, the professional relationships between the professional staff and the computing resources staff must be strong. If these two staffs cannot work well together, then attempts at cooperation with the data processing department may be a waste of time and money. If local control is elected, the home department must not take too much.

In the city of Cleveland, relations between the "development departments" and the Data Services Department were never good. Professional computer support had never been directly performed by Data Services for the City Planning Commission, for instance, and the Data Services Department issued blanket equipment recommendations without allowing for flexibility in managing different programs with potentially different requirements. All of these factors led to a choice of local control. Only much later did the Data Services Department set up liaison personnel for advising city staff on microcomputer hardware and software.

Centralization versus Decentralization

The other aspect of the large systems decision is whether or not the data base will be supported on a centralized or decentralized operating system. Figure 2.3 shows a simplified analysis of these issues. Many of these decisions cannot be made by systems designers, only because the hardware is already in place. If the hardware has not yet been acquired, then there is a good opportunity for choosing what is best without considering prior investments.

Note that Figure 2.3 distinguishes between networks and centralized systems. Networks are physical patterns of hardware that use software to link up different files in different locations or to share peripheral devices that may be accessed by numerous users. Centralization is an issue of control: control of hardware and thus control over data entry, data quality, and dissemination of data.

This area of data base design focuses not just on the selection of hardware to run the system but also on the configuration of the hardware—or how each piece of a system is connected to the others. Major questions include whether the system will run on a mainframe, a minicomputer, or a microcomputer and whether the system will be networked or whether one computer will act as a host from which others will draw all of their data. A computer checklist of questions and alternative answers is beyond the scope of this chapter (and in any case could easily be outdated by new system developments). Prospective users must raise these questions at an early point, however, and preferably with a systems designer who understands both the available hardware and software options and the existing departmental structures and data use patterns.

The Cleveland LMS project began on a very small scale with two Radio Shack microcomputers in two different departments; in terms of the scheme of Figure 2.3, the network was disintegrated and decentralized. The capability of exchanging floppy disks between machines and data through telephone connections (modem) was rarely exercised because these options were too sophisticated for the initial stage of the

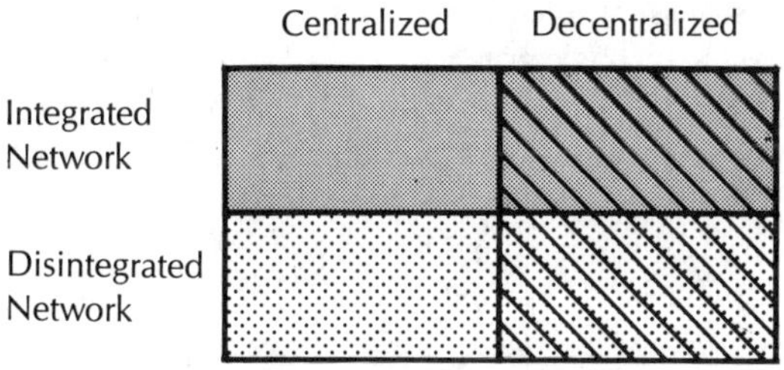

Figure 2.3. *Networks and centralization.*

overall project. Later in the project, data exchange became more frequent as basic functions began working smoothly.

Software Decisions

The decision-making process determines the basic physical configuration of the data base system to be implemented and then its nonphysical components (see Figure 2.1). The three subsets or main classifications of software include (1) commercially available packages that are generic or do a broad range of tasks in the same fashion and are called, as a group, horizontally integrated software; (2) similarly available packages that have a specific and narrow field of application but that can solve the same set of problems in different environments and are called vertically integrated software; and (3) custom programming that requires a staff member or outside vendor to write project-specific software.

Horizontal Generic Software

The proliferation of software available for a broad variety of tasks has made the selection process a difficult one. Several types of software are available for a very broad range of computer-related tasks. The main generic categories include the following:

- *Word processing:* This was one of the first areas to develop in the microcomputer field and has become the main reason that microcomputers have flourished in offices. Programs such as WordStar, Perfect Writer, Peach-Text, Scripsit, Word, and MacWrite have allowed the quick entry and editing of text and have largely automated the processing of text files. To consider a word processing software package a potential data base is possible but not likely very useful. Tabbed columns can be used to enter data, but subsequent manipulation is rudimentary.
- *Spreadsheets:* This software is responsible for the wide acceptance of microcomputers in business. It allows the user to enter data quickly in row and column formats (a basic form of data base) and to calculate relations between values or ranges of values. It also allows for quick adjustments to show the consequences of change, making it possible to perform the "what-if" analyses that are common today, particularly in financial analysis. Spreadsheets are considered the best definitive example of "horizontal" software.
- *Artificial intelligence and expert systems:* This family of programs is new to the computing field and is a powerful means of deriving computer-

based judgments from very large sets of interrelated facts and relationships. This area has not as yet been directly applied to the planning field because a high number of variables, known relationships, and types of information are needed to create even a simple expert system. Planning systems are never simple systems. While planning expert systems are not in evidence today, it is inevitable that they will begin to appear soon.[1]

• *Project management systems:* These new programs use systems methods and techniques in microcomputers to construct Gantt charts, perform PERT and network analyses, structure management by objectives, and design work flowcharts. Although these systems are not data bases, they are useful for keeping track of development work in the planning office.

• *Graphics:* This area comprises a number of subsets such as computer-aided design/computer-aided manufacturing (CAD/CAM), graphical design, and geoprocessing. Most of the recent developments in this field have resulted in specialized hardware and software because of the need for large memory storage and computational speed.

• *Data base managers:* This category of software has received some of the most intensive development work. It exploits the computer's strongest skills: accurately ordering data in various ways and at very high speeds. Microcomputer relational data bases such as dBase II and III, R-base 5000, Knowledge Man, and MS File now offer large storage capacity and sophisticated techniques for storing and manipulating the data. Because each of these data bases has characteristic strengths and limitations, the challenge is to match the software to the task at hand so that there is reasonable efficiency in processing.

Vertical Generic Software

This term refers to software developed for a narrowly defined range of activity, such as land management, as contrasted with, for example, a data base program that can be used by nearly everyone. Even though it is specialized, vertical software can be highly flexible in allowing the user to define fields, names, limits, lengths, and even processing operations as he or she sees fit. In practice, much specialized software may have both vertical and horizontal features: some functions may be of a sort that only certain professionals would use (such as the ability to digitize a map); whereas others (such as a telecommunications feature) may have extremely wide potential application.

[1]An example of a prototype expert system usable for planning purposes is the Lincoln Institute's CAESAR (Computer Aided Expert System for Analyzing Revenue), developed in 1985 by Dennis Robinson and Eugene Carter.

Custom Software

"Tailor-made" software can be written in-house or by contracting with an outside vendor. If the proposed data base has some very special and unusual needs, they may justify a custom-designed system prepared by an outside firm. However, the cost is high compared to low-cost, pre-programmed packages readily available today. Another option is to write the software using in-house staff. This can be appealing because staff members are usually intimately acquainted with the problems to be solved, but the approach can also be extremely time consuming (and costly) because the efficiencies and expertise that the outside vendor brings to the solution may not be available in-house. The initial testing and debugging phases can also be long and frustrating, whereas current commercial packages are usually bug-free by the time they are put on the market. Thus the final decision must be made between a customized product, with lengthy development time and high cost considerations, and a generic package, available immediately at low cost but perhaps not offering all the features that would be optimal.

Of course, it is possible to combine the categories mentioned above. A fully developed land management system might, in fact, employ each of the above techniques. Also, some packaged data base management programs provide a built-in programming utility so that users can design their own data handling routines.

In October 1982, when the Cleveland LMS project got underway, there was little commercial software available beyond word processing, early spreadsheets (such as VisiCalc), and simple data bases (such as Profile). This dearth of adequate computer program power was one factor that led to the adoption of SOLIR as the package that was the best available software for all the designated jobs. The city of Cleveland also acted as a "beta test site," or field test location, for this new software developed by the Lincoln Institute. This arrangement placed city staff in close contact with Institute staff, an advantageous relationship when problems arose. While the prolonged testing lengthened the data base development time, it also allowed for the concurrent use of advanced software. Such arrangements are unusual and not to be expected in general practice.

Design Decisions

In designing a data base system it is necessary to select and integrate superior software packages in order to tap the best tools for the job. If selection and rating systems are well developed, the final solutions will closely approximate the optimal solutions.

In even modest data bases, design decisions number in the hundreds, causing confusion and indecision about what to tackle first. It is best to take a structured approach, which is what we will do here: within each topic we will work from the general to the specific. Thus, we begin with considerations of what the data base will be used for, what general form it will take, what coding conventions will be used, and the like. It should be noted that many of the decisions will have already been limited by the decision making at the higher levels discussed above. The topics discussed here include links back to the goals above, scope and integration, files and records, and data elements or fields. Many other levels could be considered, but these emphasize the key points.

Linking Back to Previous Decision Steps

The last of the nonphysical aspects of the information system is the set of decisions that comprise the actual system design. It is here that decisions are made about how the final data base system will satisfy the policy goals, be stored easily in the designated hardware, and efficiently use the chosen software.

The first design consideration is the purpose the data base will serve. If the system has been designated a policy objective from the top, then other main policy goals may well be established at the same time. However, if systems are being proposed at the departmental or operational levels (in a "bottom-up" fashion), then such goals need to be carefully worked out. Most planning data bases begin with some set or subset of parcel-based information, but there can be literally hundreds of applications, such as the analysis of transportation networks, a demographic study of a neighborhood, or a choropleth (thematic) map of a region.

Not all applications are possible if critical elements are missing from the data base. For example, unless a parcel's centroid coordinates are stored, it will not be possible to determine automatically the larger geographic entity (such as voting ward) it belongs to and thereby aggregate parcel data to the next higher geographic level.

Regardless of the data base substance, the need to gather data, enter them, check for accuracy, and generate reports from them will be constant. The main question to ask is whether the major policy goals have been satisfied conceptually. The follow-up questions focus on whether the designated hardware and software are compatible with each other and the main project goals.

This phase of the design is general but nonetheless important. One of the best ways to ensure data base design issues will be linked to higher policy goals is to develop a system that reiterates through three loops—planning, implementation, and evaluation. If explicit implementation and evaluation (or monitoring) stages are established at the beginning—along with a compliance mechanism—managers are forced to assess and adjust their work regularly. Ideally, a number of critical points should be identified throughout the project that will allow for midcourse corrections and hence timely improvements in the system.

In the Cleveland LMS project, an annual reporting mechanism was created to ensure that policy makers could easily follow the progress of development and that various staff members working on isolated portions could relate their work to the project as a whole. Because this was a first effort at data base design, the project group kept reviewing the goals, particularly since they had been established in general terms at the outset.

Project Scope and Integration

Project scope has a decisive influence on the critical elements of the data base. Some of the key questions to answer include the following: Will the project be for long-term departmental support, or is it for short-term research or testing purposes? Will the data base have a mapping capability? What are the statistical requirements of the data collected? Will the data base include project management aspects, or will it include only land-related data? Will it be a land management system or something else with more specific goals?

Note that some of the broad questions of scope posed here were also asked above at the broader policy levels: the key questions are addressed, in very similar terms, at all levels. This is an example of top-down and bottom-up planning occurring simultaneously. The data base designer also needs to consider some of the following issues related to integration:

- How and by whom will the data be used? Possible users at various points in the system will include those who *generate* the data, those who *maintain* it, and those who *use* it for decision support. The data base designer will give careful thought to these categories and to the ways in which they each link to one another.
- What will be the main applications of the data base? Will it require search and retrieval, indexing and sorting, the manipulation of statistics, or straight reporting of data lists? Will it employ summarizing techniques by geographic regions, table counts, graphs, maps, or examples?
- How will the main objectives of the project be satisfied? What are the main systems issues? Will there be a requirement for holistic approaches; real-time access features; multiple data entry points or stations; interactive data bases; or data exchange by direct connection, by

modem, by exchanging disks, or by sharing a hard disk? Does data exchange need to take place in real time or as periodic updates? Is there a requirement for a local area network (LAN)?

The scope of the Cleveland project was well defined through the project approval stage, particularly since granting agencies were involved with start-up funding. The foundations required careful assurance that the project was practical and worthwhile. In the matter of integration, part of the purpose of the project was to test the amount of integration possible among the "development departments."

Files and Records

Files are the key elements of a data base. The design team must fully understand particular design goals because, after a commitment is made to a specific file structure, it becomes very expensive to change the structure.

A main consideration in designing data bases is the matter of scale. There are essentially four levels of scale on which to base a land-related system: *architectural, parcel, street,* and *zone.* These are not strict divisions, but they ought to remind the data base planner that scale has consequences for data gathering, measurement (and measurement error), statistical manipulation, and file compatibility.

Some techniques for ensuring good data base design come from the long and painful experience of those who have made costly mistakes. Therefore, it is a good idea to try to incorporate:

Common parcel entity identifiers to tie current and future files together

Common abbreviations that are standardized across a whole jurisdiction

Geocodes that have, if not a standard scale, at least a standardized conversion mechanism

Standard procedures for unusual situations (for example, "no data" and "bad data" indicators with common coding conventions)

Decisions should be made at this stage whether to incorporate data that are useful but already exist elsewhere (in coded or raw form). The main caution is to avoid accepting outside data without first checking for accuracy and reliability. Some data sources will be available by computer-to-computer communications, while other data may have to be key entered. Sources include tables of raw data from books and manuals, departmental line data, external agency data such as census data, or data from a dedicated field survey. Data may be manually transliterated or may be available in machine-readable form.

The design of each specific project within the Cleveland LMS is too complex to relate here, but the City Planning Commission may be contacted for further information. The structure of the various Cleveland data bases is given in detail in the appropriate manual and may be obtained for the cost of reproduction.

Data Elements or Fields

More fundamental than the source of a data base is the content. Here we are concerned with the individual cell values of the data base, which, of course, represent fundamental data sources. If not well thought out at this stage, the data may not convey the correct information or have the power to support later analysis needs. Suppose, for example, that a data base is built with *parcel number* as the key identifier for each record. If the design team simply records the parcel number exactly as the manual system has recorded it, it may be impossible to modify the file structure if some duplication or overlap in numbers is later discovered. In addition, parcel numbers often do not have any implicit structure because they were assigned in a nonsystematic order, but for current analysis one may want to classify parcels in a way that identifies their position in space (by grouping together blocks, neighborhoods, or census tracts). If provision is made for a future suffix to be added, for instance, the problem just illustrated can be avoided. "Garbage in—garbage out" is a familiar phrase in computer circles. As true as that is, it somewhat obscures the fact that good input can still lead to bad output, which in turn can lead to incorrect analytic conclusions. Therefore, data error checking technique is necessary to good design. Each data category has limitations on its uses, particularly in statistical manipulations and geoprocessing. Care must be taken not to give data elements any properties that they do not have.

Every data base is constrained in size. It is therefore important to estimate its final projected size accurately by knowing the limitations of field length, number of fields allowed, maximum record length, and file size measured in number of records. A data base is really a matrix of rows and columns of varying lengths. If the individual records are long, then the number of records that can be held by any given data base will be less. Designing at this level requires attention to fine detail and ability to see how all the data elements will eventually interact with one another.

Finally, there are some important questions about the general availability and quality of data to be collected locally. Have the intended data ever been collected before? If data have been collected over a long period of time, in what condition is the data base and can it be easily captured? Are all records equally reliable? How do you choose between what gets included in the new data base and what gets left to be archived in a manual or microfilmed format? How complete are the records that exist? Are there "holes" in the data files? Are newer records more important than ones collected some years ago? Are some records inherently more important than others? These questions have no fixed answers and can be resolved only by a planning professional armed with much practical experience and accumulated wisdom.

Key Data Base Design Considerations

The issues raised here illustrate that implementing effective data bases is a difficult task (see the condensed checklist at the end of this chapter). Furthermore, it is one that is evolving from a period in which planning-related information flowed from the subjective evaluations of planners rather than objective, rule-guided methods. Good public policy decision making requires a sound data base that yields useful output only after the application of seasoned professional judgment.

The four levels of major decision steps for data bases (systems, hardware, software, design) lead from general to specific design issues. The problem definition and project design tasks are the heavy front end of the process and must be patiently carried out before the easier segments are attempted. It is dangerous to rush into large projects and design "on the fly."

The challenge planners face is to develop data bases that are simple to design, test, and implement; that prove to be useful to internal and external users; and that can be transported to other similar environments for data exchange, compatibility, and testing. If these objectives are achieved, the result will be a family of planning data bases that allows for a free exchange of information about land use management and policy—a goal to which all planners must subscribe.

Checklist for Data Base Design

Systems

- Has the project the endorsement of the three levels of management: policy, departmental, operational?
- Has responsibility for the design and planning, implementation, and evaluation been properly assigned and agreed to?
- What are the sources of funding, and what amounts have been agreed on?
- What staff members have been assigned to the project, and has each person understood and agreed to the associated tasks?
- Has a work plan with key dates been written and reviewed?

Hardware

- Is the data base to be administered by the data processing department, or is it to be under local control?
- Is a network required for this data base? What form is it going to take?
- Is the data base to be centralized or decentralized? What are the reasons?

Software

- Have all the possible "horizontally integrated" software packages been reviewed for applicability?
- Have all the possible "vertically integrated" software packages been reviewed for applicability?
- Is there a real need for custom programming in this data base? If so, will it be done in-house or contracted out?

Design

- Have the main features of the data base been determined in terms of policy objectives, hardware, and software?
- Have links been made back to the higher policy levels?
- Are the scope and integration of the project assessed correctly?
- Have files and records been designed to accommodate all necessary information?
- Have data elements received adequate treatment?
- Is the data base key defined "tightly" and unambiguously?
- Have error checking mechanisms, such as random data checks or exception listings, been built in?
- Have outside sources of data been checked for accuracy and availability?
- Have internal sources of data been assessed for volume, age, accuracy, currency, and any other significant factors?

3

Neighborhood Monitoring Using Microcomputers

Rolf Goetze

As the advent of microcomputers greatly extends the range of urban planners' capabilities, creating an appropriate data base usually looms as a major and costly challenge. Among the most productive, cost-effective applications therefore are those that do not require the development of new data bases but utilize existing sources of urban information that are regularly updated—such as assessors' files, fire records, and building permit data. Some major social problems, such as the search for new policies to foster more affordable housing, can be attacked with newly emerging microcomputer systems using existing local government data.

Realizing that a closer understanding of actual housing market dynamics would lead to better strategies for housing preservation and revitalization, New Haven several years ago began a neighborhood listening program, using microcomputers to handle data. Neighborhood listening is field interviewing to gather the perceptions of residents, but it may of course also reveal fundamental income, employment, and crime problems (or even excessive dependence on public assistance), which housing strategies alone cannot address.

Improving on its arson warning and prevention system, New Haven devised a parcel-based system for tracking such factors as code violations, tax delinquency, title turnover, and condominium conversions, along with program participation. This chapter summarizes what has been learned to date from New Haven's initiatives to create a Land Use Information System (LUIS).

Why Monitor Neighborhood Change?

Studies in Boston and elsewhere have shown that motivation to maintain property is often a more critical factor in neighborhood preservation than purely economic concepts of affordability (Goetze 1979). When community residents and owners lack confidence in their neighborhood's future, traditional public assistance programs do not restore community self-reliance but often instill an increasing dependence on more subsidies and assistance. In many marginal neighborhoods, new approaches can boost and restore confidence at far less cost in public resources than recent stop-gap loan, grant, and infill development programs.

While conventional wisdom has accepted a simple neighborhood continuum that ranks housing conditions on a scale from good to poor, this oversimplifies matters. A matrix relating housing conditions to market perceptions is more useful (Figure 3.1). Neighborhood classifications cannot be reduced to one-dimensional indicator levels of good, fair, or poor, but they can be located conceptually on this matrix in order to differentiate appropriate policy treatments.

Perceived demand for housing in each area—something to which real estate interests are acutely sensitive—is a useful proxy for neighborhood confidence. As confidence in the future of a neighborhood improves, demand firms up. This unleashes the latent efforts of residents and many private interests to play supporting roles, making improve-

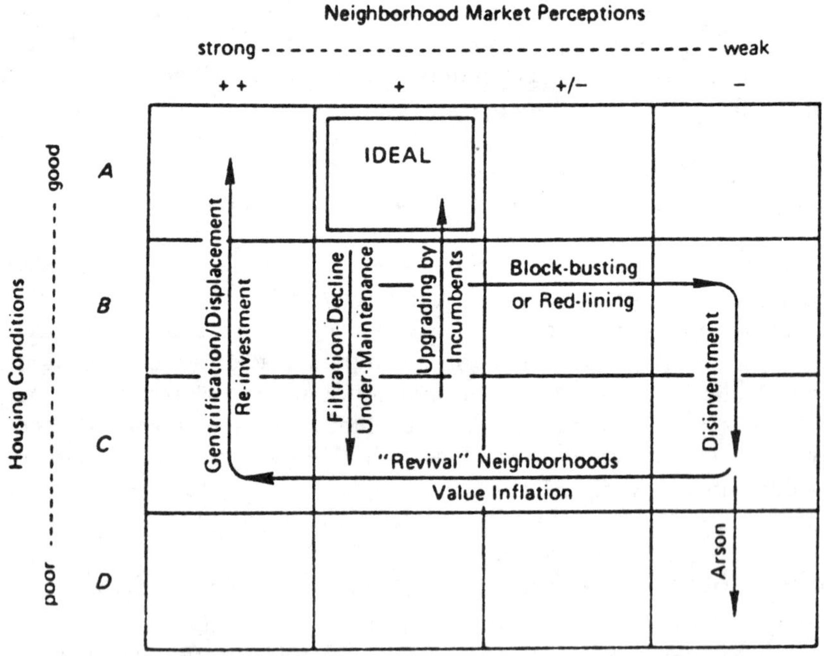

Figure 3.1. *The matrix of housing dynamics* (Source: *Goetze,* Understanding Neighborhood Change, *1979*).

ments long held back by the conviction that individuals "couldn't make a difference anyway" and that lack of care "didn't matter."

Neighborhood dynamics must be accurately understood before they can be improved to promote greater self-reliance. Change enters neighborhoods in various ways before it becomes visible: through market imbalances (increased vacancies when supply exceeds demand, or creation of accessory apartments and condo conversions when demand exceeds supply) and through turnover to new ownership (sales to inexperienced operators who may become disinvestors in a glut, or gentrification and upscale improvements where housing seems dear). The objective is to identify those factors (ideally, indicators already in the public record, like tax delinquency) that can be most easily monitored over time and yet that reflect the salient changes early enough to enable planners to intervene at the margins—before, once again, they are called on to address the latest unexpected "problem."

Purpose should guide the design of any monitoring system. Costs of obtaining reliable, consistent data should then discipline the efforts. In order to devise more equitable and cost-effective programs and market interventions, policy makers need to know more fully what is actually going on in each neighborhood and how public interventions can influence and alter market dynamics.

These requirements suggest several useful types of questions regarding neighborhood change. First, neighborhood monitoring can address some general market symptoms:

What is the actual rate of abandonment? Is it slowing or growing?

What type of properties are deteriorating most rapidly? Where?

How are abandonment patterns shifting, spreading, or shrinking?

Where are conditions stable and improving?

What types of properties are involved in suspicious fires?

What types of properties seem immune to deterioration? Where?

Which types of properties seem to lead in neighborhood change?

Beyond such general issues, monitoring neighborhood conditions can get "beneath the surface" and help to identify the actual causes of change, trace the impacts of interventions, validate proxies for many aspects that cannot be directly measured, and improve our basic understanding of the housing market system. A neighborhood monitoring system should be able to relate market symptoms to one another to provide a preliminary understanding of neighborhood dynamics. Typical questions here might include the following:

When newcomers enter a neighborhood, is it their homes or those of established residents that first undergo change?

Compared to resident owners, are absentee investors better or worse in regard to maintenance? Does scale of ownership make a difference?

How often do resident owners move out but retain title as owners? Is this more prevalent in some areas than others?

Where are there cases of assisted fix-up or new development, and what is their impact on surrounding properties?

What are the general sales price trends, and how are these reflected in sales/assessment ratios? Do these ratios differ by neighborhood or vary by property, and do they shift over time?

Can available data on financing practices (such as government insured mortgages, bank foreclosures, and quit claim deeds) serve as early warning indicators of neighborhood change?

Still another type of question reveals the accuracy of existing governmental measures of change:

Do code violations reliably reflect actual conditions?

How accurate are city records regarding dwelling counts?

How closely are liens, tax arrears, and records of fires associated with deteriorating conditions?

Do city records accurately track changes in use like accessory apartments, condominium conversions, and demolitions?

There are many reasons for monitoring change. However, neighborhoods are complex and many faceted, so the actual determinants of change (such as decisions to disinvest or commit arson-for-profit) may not be directly measurable. Deciding to monitor in order to better understand underlying motivations involves many tradeoffs and compromises. We need inexpensive proxies—so-called unobtrusive indicators.

In the ideal or "healthy" neighborhood it is axiomatic that properties are in good condition and that vacancies, housing and building code violations, tax arrears, fires, and property crimes are minimized. Each of these terms can be considered a *factor* or *proxy* related individually to every property or parcel in the information base. "Soft" factors such as conditions, if used, must be recorded in ways that assure consistency—so that separate observers concur in their ratings. (To have a property's condition described as fair is of little use if another observer judges the same property to be good or poor.)

Considering the matrix in Figure 3.1, a neighborhood is also judged healthy when market dynamics are seen as stable—that is, when supply matches demand, when property values are just keeping pace with inflation, and when the length of time on the market of listings for sale is reasonable. Either too little or too much demand, revealed in stagnating or soaring property values, indicates market problems that can undermine neighborhood stability. These proxies of neighborhood conditions and market dynamics suggest a host of factors that can monitor change. Note that their primary purpose is to indicate current states. Repeated consistently over time, they also become useful for establishing rates and patterns of change. However, even if 100 percent accurate, they are only proxies and do not directly reveal the underlying causes of change.

In sum, the primary purpose of neighborhood monitoring is to determine objectively, through inexpensive measures of "stocks and flows" (or "states and rates") where there is improvement and stability and where there is deterioration. Consistent, parcel-based measures regularly repeated over time are most suited to provide such information, but how are these conditions best measured?

Monitoring Indicators

Census data are useful for contextual background, particularly in making comparisons among census tracts. Factors such as the following are very revealing:

Stock composition (one-unit, two-unit, three- to four-unit, five-plus-unit structures)

Tenure (owner-occupied, renter-occupied, vacant, and for-sale units)

Median values of owner-occupied units, and median contract rents

Mobility (residence in 1980 of persons over age 5 in 1985)

Percentage of minorities (by race, linguistic group, or ancestry)

Percentage of households under the poverty threshold

Household composition (families, female-headed, nonfamily, elderly)

New stock additions since 1970

These communicate best when analyzed in ways discussed below. Initially, they can be effectively displayed in tables by listing tracts down the side and critical factors across the top. Such tables also can be designed to reveal changes from one measurement year to another (this, of course, requires some simple subtraction and division).

While helpful, census data are nevertheless inadequate as monitoring tools for two basic reasons: (1) they are gathered only every ten years, which means that short-term changes and turnarounds in trends cannot be detected, and (2) they are aggregated by geographic blocks and tracts to provide confidentiality. This prevents researchers from learning how several characteristics associate and influence adjoining properties. For example, in what ways are such factors as property types, conditions, and values interlinked with mobility, race, and tenure?

Much more can be done with city records collected at the *parcel level.* A wealth of parcel-based data is already in the public domain, regularly collected by city agencies that perform functions such as assessing and collecting taxes, inspecting buildings, issuing permits, preventing fires, and dealing with crime. These elements of useful information are collected separately and stored by various city departments, on anything from cards and manila folders to sophisticated computer and microfiche systems. Microcomputers now make it possible to bring together such dispersed data in order to examine specific factors in context, identify changes, and analyze underlying patterns, but first there must be an unambiguous, generally acceptable system for referring to each property. Address (or map, block, and parcel number) must be clear and logical. Confusion in street numbering (such as numbers like 67a, 67½, 67–71) and missing addresses for corner lots and vacant parcels must be resolved to a simple, consistent format.

The most appropriate measures for a neighborhood monitoring system are those proxies identified above that not only serve to compare the actual with the optimal situation but also can be obtained without great cost. Parcel-based information regularly collected by public agencies for their own purposes is most convenient. Because such agencies use it, it is systematically updated and likely to be accurate.

Field information regarding conditions and actual dwelling counts, at least on a sampling basis, is essential to determine what the city records actually mean and the extent to which they can serve as proxies. What is the relationship between parcels, buildings, and units at a given address? A physical confirmation of "what is really out there" also inspires confidence in city records—and a mismatch suggests useful administrative changes. Are there instances where city records indicate the presence of a building where there now is a vacant lot, or a residential property that now contains a store? Doorbell counts often reveal such significant discrepancies. What about physical conditions (need of paint or lack of storm windows)? Lack of storm windows, for example, is an unobtrusive indicator of energy waste. Field investigations show it is a useful proxy for estimating the size of a possible weatherization program and the potential costs and benefits of providing caulking, attic insulation, and storm windows.

Standardized criteria monitored regularly by parcel in pilot areas (such as sash conditions and storm windows) can quickly reveal trends toward either improvement or disinvestment. The most valuable data are not necessarily those that are most accurate but rather those that simply are repeated regularly and consistently.

Once suitable proxies have been selected for testing and a consistent address base is agreed on, it becomes possible to start creating an effective neighborhood monitoring system of the type outlined above. Unfortunately, there is no direct one-to-one correspondence between any one question and individual data elements because the latter are only proxies. If they are used together, however, a valuable synergy occurs, enabling researchers to grasp the underlying dynamics and confirm them through complementary field research using a few probing questions to those most familiar with the areas.

The New Haven Land Use Information System

Phase 1

With the above considerations in mind, the development administrator of the city of New Haven decided to test the use of city and field data in devising better housing policies and market interventions for its neighborhoods. New Haven purchased its first microcomputer, a TRS-80 Model II, in June 1982 in order to test the suitability of the Lincoln Institute's SOLIR software for urban analytical research. SOLIR is a generic system providing a variety of software elements that permit the user to design data bases, enter and maintain the data (electronically or manually), and perform various statistical, mapping, and other computational activities. It also allows the user to display the results on a computer screen, printer, or plotter and to estimate property values, identify comparables, and transfer data between computers.

The SOLIR program was tested to determine its effectiveness in storing and analyzing extensive parcel-based information in targeted areas of the city. Eight study areas were selected where one- to four-family dwelling units prevailed. Each was chosen to be both internally homogeneous in housing quality and market dynamics and at the same time prototypical of a different type of housing market in New Haven, or cell in our matrix (Figure 3.1). Data were gathered on 1,487 parcels, representing some 6 percent of New Haven's housing stock. The study team then decided to ignore rooming houses, multifamily structures, and vacant lots in order to focus on comparisons among the dwellings containing one to four families. This left 1,298 parcels.

Statistical tables generated through SOLIR clearly reflect neighborhood differences. Tables 3.1, 3.2, and 3.3 are presented here only to

Table 3.1
Housing Conditions by Neighborhood Study Area (Parcel Count)

	Neighborhood Study Area								
	1	*2*	*3*	*4*	*5*	*6*	*7*	*8*	*Total*
Good condition	120	159	141	151	89	52	102	265	1,079
Minor defects	1	24	4	14	37	11	42	2	135
Major defects	0	6	0	1	8	0	23	0	38
Dilapidated	0	0	1	0	2	17	8	0	28
Vacant lot	0	13	1	0	1	1	2	0	18
Totals	121	202	147	166	137	81	177	267	1,298

show how significant contrasts among the study areas are revealed in such SOLIR tables, which are two-way frequency distributions. Table 3.1 displays the actual parcel distributions by condition for the eight study areas, while Table 3.2 shows the same data in column percentages, pointing out more clearly the relative conditions. Table 3.3 introduces a third factor, owner occupancy (identified by comparing the names in the residential directory with the assessor's owner of record), which looks bewildering but on closer inspections suggests the importance of resident ownership to housing conditions across the study areas.

Simple two-way tables like these provide an essential base for more sophisticated analyses. Creating a number of such tables lays an analytic foundation or base, revealing the relationships between property types, tenure, condition, and age—all by neighborhoods or census tracts. For each such table, their associated percentage distributions—shown as the row and column sums—reveal the norms for the city. These provide some preliminary reference measures for comparing the composition of different areas and submarkets.

Table 3.2
Housing Conditions by Neighborhood Study Area (Percentage of Parcel Distribution)

	Neighborhood Study Area								
	1	*2*	*3*	*4*	*5*	*6*	*7*	*8*	*Total*
Good condition	99.2	78.7	95.9	91.0	65.0	64.2	57.6	99.3	83.1
Minor defects	0.8	11.9	2.7	8.4	27.0	13.6	23.7	0.7	10.4
Major defects	0.0	3.0	0.0	0.6	5.8	0.0	13.0	0.0	2.9
Dilapidated	0.0	0.0	0.7	0.0	1.5	21.0	4.5	0.0	2.2
Vacant lot	0.0	6.4	0.7	0.0	0.7	1.2	1.1	0.0	1.4
Totals	100.0	100.0	100.0	100.0	100.0	100.0	100.0	100.0	100.0

Table 3.3
Housing Conditions in Relation to Owner Occupancy, by Neighborhood Study Area

	Neighborhood Study Area								
	1	*2*	*3*	*4*	*5*	*6*	*7*	*8*	*Total*
Good condition									
All parcels	120	159	141	151	89	52	102	265	1,079
Owner-occupied	84	74	72	54	20	10	16	179	509
% owner-occupied	70	47	51	36	22	19	16	68	47
Minor defects									
All parcels	1	24	4	14	37	11	42	2	135
Owner-occupied	0	7	2	3	5	1	8	0	26
% owner-occupied	0	29	50	21	14	9	19	0	19
Major defects									
All parcels	0	6	0	1	8	0	23	0	38
Owner-occupied	0	2	0	0	3	0	1	0	6
% owner-occupied	0	33	0	0	38	0	4	0	16
Dilapidated or vacant lot									
All parcels	0	13	2	0	3	18	10	0	46
Owner-occupied	0	3	0	0	1	6	0	0	10
% owner-occupied	0	22	0	0	33	33	0	0	22
Totals									
All parcels	121	202	147	166	137	81	177	267	1,298
Owner-occupied	84	86	74	57	29	17	25	179	551
% owner-occupied	69	43	50	34	21	21	14	67	42

Aggregating third factors in reference to these basic tables makes significantly more powerful analyses possible. For example, taking the table of property types by neighborhoods as a base for counting the number of fires associated with each cell in this table suggests which particular property types (single family units, triplexes, multifamily units, commercial units, and so forth) in which specific neighborhoods are most fire-prone. Third factors useful for aggregation in such basic tables include tenure type (ownership by resident, neighbor, or absentee), unpaid taxes and liens, code violations, and sales prices.

Data on assisted housing (both new developments and rehabilitation) by census tract, when available from city records, adds another dimension of meaning to the above tables.

One purpose of such reconnaissance research is to identify the deviates or outliers for further examination (for example, the areas with the highest and lowest rates of fires, liens, and properties in tax title) and at the same time reveal where and in which particular land uses these extremes predominate. Examining these also identifies the most appropriate critical indicators of neighborhood change.

Phase II

Success in this first microcomputer research initiative induced New Haven to embark on creating a citywide microcomputer-based Land Use Management Information System. In order to be effective, a comprehensive municipal information system must respond to the needs of many potential users. The three layers of government activities—general operations, resource management, and policy formation—have different information requirements, not only in terms of types of information but in the level of detail, accuracy, and currency of the data. Unless limited to some specialized purpose, a useful information system must meet all three types of needs. Even though the needs of the policymakers are most important, the day-to-day needs of operations level staff are the driving force that supports and sustains the entire system.

New Haven has demonstrated that data from many city agencies can be usefully integrated if one takes care to make components compatible. Getting individual agencies to coordinate and collaborate is not easy, but seeing that each gets at least its "quid pro quo" has encouraged more and more to join in (City of New Haven 1985).

New Haven's experience has led it to expand Phase II along two dimensions. The first is temporal. The use of simple, consistent data elements permits much greater research power than impressive but costly "one-off" initiatives. The basic and aggregate tables described in Table 3.4, when updated appropriately, provide the city with a much better grasp of the composition of its residential land uses, as well as a preliminary evaluation of the effectiveness of its city records for identifying trouble-prone properties. The patterns revealed over time by records of fires, tax liens, requests for permits, zoning appeals, and the like will all become more meaningful when examined in this basic context.

The second dimension is structural. A generic system of nested tables will help analysts "window in" on significant subsets of all parcels. From the superset of all residential properties, sets of one- to six-unit residential and multifamily properties can be identified. Within these, subsets can be selected that show which are resident-owned, absentee-owned, market properties, or assisted by public programs. (See columns A through G in Table 3.4.)

To identify significant patterns—such as fires, liens, tax arrears, and sales price trends—a common set of elements should be tallied for each series. Each cell identified in Table 3.4 represents an actual table displaying data by census tract. (Tables A1 through G8 are cited in Table 3.4 but are not reproduced in this book.) For example, Table A2 indicates fire rates for all parcels, Table B2 reveals fires in one- to six-family

Table 3.4
A Generic System of Nested Tables Displaying LUMIS Data by Census Tract

		Residential					
	Totals	*One- to-Four Unit*			*Multifamily*		
	All parcels by land uses	*Subtotal*	*Resident-owned*	*Absentee-owned*	*Subtotal*	*Private*	*Assisted*
3d Factor	*A*	*B*	*C*	*D*	*E*	*F*	*G*
1. Parcel count	A1	B1	C1	D1	E1	F1	G1
2. Fires	A2	B2	C2	D2	E2	F2	G2
3. Liens	A3	B3	C3	D3	E3	F3	G3
4. Tax arrears	A4	B4	C4	D4	E4	F4	—
5. Sales prices	A5	B5	C5	D5	E5	F5	—
6. Dwelling count	A6	B6	C6	D6	E6	F6	G6
7. Resident owned	—	B7	—	—	—	—	—
8. Condition	—	B8	C8	D8	E8	F8	G8
9. Market data	—	B9	C9	D9	E9	F9	—

units, and Table C2 shows fires in the resident-owned one- to six-unit parcels. Through this analytical approach, norms and deviations emerge and elements that prove to be most useful in these analyses of available data will be tracked in the future to serve as critical indicators of change. Appendix 3A elaborates on the system of nested tables suggested in Table 3.4.

Once this base is established and has been analyzed, policy makers can begin to use the system for policy applications such as estimating the cost of bringing all housing into code compliance or developing a profile of arson-prone properties and scanning the data base for others that are comparable in order to create an early warning system. Similarly, they can identify precursors to disinvestment and then monitor factors like condition, rents, mobility, tenure, and values in order to devise timely interventions aimed at averting more serious disinvestment.

This LUIS data base is designed to be largely self-maintaining—that is, it is based on integrating data already being recorded by separate agencies for their own needs. Therefore, it can regularly furnish some of the updates required for monitoring changes over time and even suggest changes in the rates of change. For indicating specific market changes, however, such agency records are generally too fragmented and incomplete in most cities. For that purpose, both time series data and some additional field and market information, maintained regularly on a sample basis, are an essential component of a land use management information system. However, the initial set of tables outlined in Appendix 3A will be helpful in determining the reliability of city data and identifying the factors that can best serve as proxies for monitoring changes over time in market dynamics and property conditions.

In order to avoid creation of too many or excessively large data tables, the periodic analyses are generally best aggregated to the census tract level. To the extent feasible, factor values should be recorded annually and measured consistently whenever possible. In monitoring, consistency is very important. Modifying the methodology to keep up with any state of the art should be strongly resisted.

Other Useful Pattern and Anomaly Identification Techniques

Rankings

Patterns in the information developed above become more evident when the computer is used to rank from top to bottom. This illustration will focus on information organized geographically, such as by study neighborhoods or census tracts, but the technique is effective for any parallel data—that is, for factors among which associations are likely. For example, when we analyze data for percentage-deteriorated in each of New Haven's twenty-eight tracts, the resulting table simply indicates the rank of each tract from lowest to highest (instead of, or in addition to, the actual values).

For ease in detecting subtler patterns in associated data, using this ranking technique, consistency in choosing the *top* and *bottom* is important. For example, long-term residency, high percentage of resident ownership, and lack of substandard conditions all tend to go together—and where they do not we may be alerted that more research may be productive.

This rank ordering serves to reveal such anomalies as unusually good conditions in rental areas, tracts with unexpectedly long-term residents who are not owners, or areas where fires do not appear to be associated with liens or deteriorated conditions. Such anomalies or departures from the ways one would expect the data to be associated provide clues to underlying forces of vitality that can be harnessed and guided by planners to induce private and community forces to do more of the fix-up.

Maps

Sorting these rankings into quintiles to identify tracts near and far from the city norm prepares the data for mapping that can communicate patterns most effectively. Using thematic mapping capabilities with the analytic routines mentioned previously can be very helpful in detecting anomalies.

Other factors that appear useful in the rankings or tables can also be displayed on maps and may stimulate many insights when posted side by side. Such factors might include the following:

- Median sales prices
- Stock composition, such as percentage of single family, three- to four-unit structures, resident-owned, multifamily, or assisted
- Percentage of parcels with fires
- Percentage of parcels with tax liens
- Census data on contract rents and single-family home prices

Changes over the decade can be shown on maps now, even before the parcel-based land use management information system is fully operational, using census data from 1970 and 1980 to reveal the quintiles of percentage of change, as suggested above. For example, in New

Haven the areas with the greatest change in minority residence, and in median sales prices and rents, experienced the most trauma. These are especially appropriate areas for further field research, to determine how well both stock and residents coped with high rates of change.

Dot or *measle* maps can also prove very revealing, once parcel-based data are on record. Maps pinpointing the incidence of certain events or situations like fires, vacancies, and significant price surges tell even more than maps aggregating such information by geographic areas like census tracts.

Individual factors mapped in isolation, however, are much less useful than seeing them superimposed as overlays on the base maps developed using quintiles, or other displays placing them in the context of abutting land uses.

Indexing and Listing

Listing specific parcels with several problem indicators (such as fires, liens, code violations, vacancies, and critical ownership) enables much more effective follow-up field research, whereas the aggregation of data concerning problems *within an area* adds little to what one could already discern from a single *windshield survey.* Analysis should begin with tracts or parcels that stand out in some way or have experienced significant change: new ownership at a remarkable price (high or low or with unusual financing), abnormal vacancy, change in number of dwellings at an address, change in condition, several liens, or several fires. At the micro level, it is useful to print out salient data on the surrounding parcels and take all this into the field to eyeball the situation and examine these parcels in their geographic context. Since condition ratings require field surveys (which may not yet have been done), these analyses can also be worked backward to determine whether city records can serve as reliable proxies for parcel-specific information regarding conditions. In trouble-prone areas, all properties with several strikes against them should be printed out. At the same time, independent field surveys should be done to evaluate the conditions of all structures in these particular areas. Then placing the two lists side by side reveals both the reliability of the city records as well as their usefulness in identifying the most trouble-prone properties and useful indicators of neighborhood change.

Summary

The preceding discussion suggests how creating an initial set of basic tables, rankings, maps, and lists can provide research tools for improving our grasp of neighborhood change and revitalization. As time series data become available, user experience will have identified the critical indicators and analyses that are most suitable, based on actual data now available or obtainable from agencies with staff engaged in daily operations. The challenge of inducing them to join in this effort to create a land use management information system is a healthy one, since autonomous agencies rarely serve their public well.

The unique strengths of parcel-specific data emerge from the preceding analyses to suggest the most effective combinations of factors for further analyses. Until now, planners have generally been limited to data aggregated in different ways—by census tracts and by school districts, political wards, and even police precincts. This prevented the detection of meaningful patterns. The resolution of details was not adequate to reveal anomalies that serve to liberate planning from conventional wisdom. Broadly blaming change on slumlords, on redlining by bankers, on racist steering by brokers, or even on speculation by gentrifiers is not useful for policy formulation. When newcomers enter a neighborhood and deterioration results, *what actually takes place, step by step?* Parcel-based, time series data make it possible to form and then confirm or refute specific hunches.

This increase in the power of resolution afforded by dealing with parcel-based data is analogous to obtaining an electron microscope after using only a weak optical microscope. However, just as with an electron microscope, neither time nor resources permit one to "point it everywhere." The preceding systematic types of research—developing basic tables, rankings, and maps in order to identify norms, extremes, and anomalies—serve to reveal the most fertile areas for further inquiry.

William Alonso, a noted land use planner, remarked years ago that "second derivatives"—changes in the rate of change—contain the most significant information for planning and policy formulation. Whereas such basic statistics as the number of units, households, permits, liens, or fires are necessary, the information becomes notably more useful when changes in these quantities over time are revealed.

The data become much more powerful when they permit detection of small divergencies from basic trends in different geographic areas. For example, they may reveal that in certain areas the trend toward increasing resident ownership has stopped or that the decline in the number of fires per neighborhood has reversed. This alerts policymakers to potentially significant underlying shifts, enabling them to aim their field research in more productive directions.

Data collected repeatedly, *and the same way each time,* are best suited for revealing such changes. In contrast to the complete information needed for day-to-day operations (where any inaccuracies are disconcerting), information for policy purposes can be gleaned from many sources that collect the same measures consistently over time, even if only on a sample basis. Such sophisticated analyses, however, become possible only when comparable data, gathered consistently for several years, becomes available. The first steps are to establish a useful data base, composed of regularly updated information, that can then provide the reference points for monitoring change.

Fortunately, compared to the direct expense of even a few Section 8 commitments, the cost of developing such sensitive information systems is modest due to the tumbling prices in microcomputers. Within a few years, planners in some cities like New Haven will gain up-to-date fingertip access to the current pulse of change in neighborhood markets via the desktop microcomputer, using sensitive proxy indicators of neighborhood dynamics and change. Their rewards will lie in a greater mastery over the policies used to guide such change.

Appendix 3A. A Generic System of Nested Tables

The following descriptions and tables illustrate the types of data tables useful for monitoring neighborhood change in any municipality.

The Master Table (Table 3.4)

Each cell in the matrix in Table 3.4 represents a potential table or cluster of tables. Column A is based on all parcels in the data base. It is the sum of columns B (one- to four-unit residential), E (multifamily), and an additional factor (not shown) representing nonresidential parcels. Column B in turn is the sum of C and D. Column E is the sum of F and G.

Each row represents a series of tables based on a particular attribute. Thus, in tables based on row 1 the units are parcels; in tables based on row 2 the units are fires; and so on for each row. One can also create parallel tables with the units expressed as percentages (indicated by an *a* after the table number), as median values *(b)*, and so on.

Actual tables are not shown, since their cell values would be illustrative only; however, the captions listed below under "List of Table Contents" indicates the content of each table derivable from Table 3.4. To illustrate, consider the tables in Column A (all parcels).

Parcel Count

Table A1, Property Types by Census Tracts, is the primary table displaying the particular land use composition of each tract. A companion, Table A1a, can be constructed, showing the same information in row and column percentages. Such a table better reveals both the distribution of land uses and the similarities and contrasts between individual tracts.

Similar tables can be created in the same display format using software capable of aggregating third factors and calculating percentage of aggregate value, mean, count, and percentage of count. (Table 3.3 is an example of such a table.)

Table A1
Property Types by Census Tracts

Census Tract	*Residential 1–4 d.u.*	*Apartment 5+ d.u.*	*Condo*	*Exempt*	*Commercial*	*Industrial*	*Utility*	*Total*
1 CBD								
2 Church St.								
3 City Point								
•								
•								
•								
•								
•								
•								
28 Morris Cove								
City total								

Fires

Tables A2a and A2b explore the incidence of fires. Table A2a focuses on the percentage of parcels shown in base Table A1 with any fires causing damage. Table A2b concentrates on the median number of fires per parcel with any fires. This reveals both the areas and property types most fire prone—and sets the stage for a subsequent printout of the 200 parcels with the most fires, or all parcels having experienced more than three fires.

Liens

Tables A3a and A3b similarly explore the incidence of liens. Again, Table A3a focuses on the percentage of parcels with any liens, and Table A3b on the median number of liens per parcel with any liens.

Tax Title

Tables A4a and A4b likewise examine the patterns of tax arrears. Table A4a displays the percentage of parcels with any tax arrears, and Table A4b shows the median amount per parcel with any arrears.

Sales and Median Prices

Tables A5a, A5b, and A5c are related to sales. Table A5a identifies the percentage of parcels on base Table A1 sold at least once in the past year. Table A5b shows the median sales price for the properties sold, separated by land use types. Table A5c displays the median values resulting from calculating the ratio of individual sale price to assessment for the properties sold.

Summary Counts of Residential Units

To reconcile these statistics with U.S. Census tract level data involving dwelling unit and household counts, Tables A6a, A6b, and A6c provide residential overviews. Table A6a reveals the total number of dwelling units in each tract by property type. Table A6b shows the percentage of all parcels in Table A1 with any residential units, and Table A6c provides the mean number of dwellings per parcel for those parcels with any dwellings.

More Detailed Residential Analyses

Consistency in formatting the data is as important for detecting and understanding change as using information gathered the same way each time. Therefore, the tables in series B, C, and D should all use the format shown in Table B, and series E, F, and G should follow the format of Table E.

Series B, C, and D: One- to Six-Unit Residential Subset

These tables are formatted to parallel the A series to enable easy comparisons. However, these tables show only the one- to six-unit residential parcels, separating out the number of dwelling units per parcel into individual columns. As a result, the total column, far right, represents only the first column in Table A1 (if *residential* has been defined as one- to six-units).

Table B1 lays out the total number of parcels in each tract by number of dwelling units per parcel, serving as secondary base table. (Zero dwelling units means a vacant lot classed as residential, whereas vacant structures should be tallied under the appropriate stock type.)

Again, a companion, Table B1a, shows the row and column percentages, revealing both the varying composition of the residential stock by tract and the

Table B
Tables for All 1- to 6-Unit Residential Parcels

Census Tract	*0 d.u.*	*1 d.u.*	*2 d.u.*	*3–4 d.u.*	*Subtotal 1–4 d.u.*	*5–6 d.u.*	*Total 1–6 d.u.*
1 CBD							
2 Church St.							
3 City Point							
•							
•							
•							
•							
•							
•							
28 Morris Cove							
City total							

Table E
Tables for All Multifamily Residential Parcels

Census Tract	*5–6 d.u.*	*7–9 d.u.*	*10–19 d.u.*	*20–49 d.u.*	*50–99 d.u.*	*100+ d.u.*	*Total*
1 CBD							
2 Church St.							
3 City Point							
•							
•							
•							
•							
•							
•							
28 Morris Cove							
City total							

overall distribution across the city of particular stock types like single-family and three- and four-unit structures. The totals by row and column again furnish the norms for comparison.

Third factor aggregations are repeated for the B series, using the same factors as the A series, *fires* (Tables B2a and B2b), *liens* (Tables B3a and B3b), *tax title* (Tables B4a and B4b), and *sales and median prices* (Tables B5a, B5b, and B5c).

The following additional information is also to be displayed in these third-factor aggregations:

Dwelling counts: Table B6 tallies the number of dwelling units.

Resident ownership: Table B7 shows the percentage of all parcels on base Table B1 that are resident owned.

Condition: Table B8 shows the percentage of all parcels in base Table B1 that are in deteriorating or worse condition.

Market data: Table B9a shows the percentage of sales in the last year that were at arm's length by stock type and tract. Table B9b shows the median sales prices of properties sold in arm's-length transactions. Table B9c shows the median sales price/assessment ratios calculated from the most recent sales price of each property sold.

If information on *length of time on the market* and *asking/sales price ratios* is obtainable, even only for a significant fraction of all sales, then such data should also be displayed in similar tables for comparison.

Series C and D: One- to Six-Unit Properties, Resident- and Nonresident-Owned

These two series are a matched set—that is, parcels appearing on base Table B1 will reappear in either series C or D. Their purpose is to enable policy makers to differentiate situations that are either better or worse than average and to focus even more closely on the specific areas, property type, and tenure situations that are likely to have fires, liens, tax arrears, and deteriorating conditions.

Tables C1 to C9 and D1 to D9 are to be created in parallel with the preceding sets, to enable side-by-side inspection for patterns.

This set of "nested" tables just described provides a generic approach for seeking out patterns embedded in existing, parcel-level data. The same basic approach is useful to explore for similar patterns in multifamily residential stock. This time, however, the comparisons are between private and assisted housing.

Series E, F, and G: Multifamily Residential Subsets

The various multifamily analyses examining private (F) and assisted housing (G) are again done in parallel and have the same unit breakouts, for consistency. Six, ten, twenty, fifty, and 100 units per parcel are suggested break-points, as shown in Table E.

The assessor's designation for apartment (seen in Table A) is used as a proxy for private multifamily in Table E; and the indicator for tax exempt property in Table A is used for assisted housing in Table G.

Tables E1, F1, and G1 show the respective amounts of multifamily property types by census tract, and, once again, Tables E1a, F1a, and G1a translate the same data into row and column percentages.

Using these tables as basic formats to display property types by census tract, parallel special tables aggregating third factors are again created. As far as possible, the same conventions are used for these factors as in the A through D series.

More detailed analysis is appropriate to detect patterns linked to special types of assistance—such as Section 8 existing housing, public housing projects, co-ops, 221(d)(3)'s and 202's—to the extent that these data can be added to the parcel records.

In some instances (such as Section 8 existing housing), it is suitable to treat this as another third-factor aggregate count, creating Tables F7 and G7. In others (such as public housing versus 221(d)(3)'s and other private, assisted developments), "nested, complementary" tables are more appropriate, as was done for series C and D, as well as F and G, above.

List of Table Contents

Property Tables (All Residential Types)

1. Basic tables (illustrated in Table A)

   Table A1. Property Types by Census Tracts (numbers = parcel counts)

   Table A1a. Property Types by Census Tracts (same data by row and column percentage distributions; numbers = percentage)

Third-factor aggregate tables (also based on Table A above)

2. Fires

   Table A2a. Percentage of Parcels with Damaging Fires by Census Tracts (numbers = percentage of all parcels in each cell; row and column percentage distributions should also be developed where useful)

   Table A2b. Median Number of Fires Per Parcel with Fire Damage by Census Tract (numbers = respective medians for each cell)

3. Property liens

   Table A3a. Percentage of Parcels with Any Liens by Census Tract (a threshold of liens over $100 may be advisable)

   Table A3b. Median Number of Liens Per Parcel with Any Liens by Census Tract

4. Tax arrears

   Table A4a. Percentage of Parcels with Any Tax Arrears by Census Tract

   Tale A4b. Median Amount of Tax Arrears in Relation to Parcels in Arrears by Census Tract

5. Sales and median prices

   Table A5a. Percentage of Parcels Sold at Least Once by Census Tract

   Table A5b. Median Sales Price Per Parcel for Properties Sold by Census Tract (based on the most recent sales price)

   Table A5c. Median Sales/Assessment Ratio of Sold Parcels by Census Tract

6. Dwelling count

   Table A6. Total Number of Dwelling Units by Census Tract (average number of dwellings per parcel would also be created within this table)

Tables Monitoring Change

When time series data become available, the *same* third factors that emerged above as most useful are aggregated to develop the following:

Table A1. Absolute Change in Parcel Count and Land Uses by Census Tract (percentage of change in count may be useful as well)

Table A2. Percentage of Change (+/−) in Number of Parcels with Fires by Census Tract

Table A3. Percentage of Change (+/−) in Number of Parcels with Liens by Census Tract

Table A4. Percentage of Change in Number of Parcels in Tax Arrears by Census Tract

Table A5. Percentage of Change (+/−) in Median Sales Prices by Census Tract

Table A6. Absolute Change (+/−) in Dwelling Count by Census Tract (percentage change in count may be useful as well)

Series B, C, and D follow the same format, using B as the base table. Series E, F, and G also follow this format, but use Table E as the base table.

Property Tables (One- to Six-Unit Residential Properties)

1. Basic tables (see Table B)

   Table B1. Property Types by Census Tracts (numbers = parcel counts)

   Table B1a. Property Types by Census Tracts (same data by row and column percentage distributions; numbers = percentage)

   Third-factor aggregate tables (also based on Table B above)

2. Fires

   Table B2a. Percentage of Parcels with Damaging Fires by Census Tracts (numbers = percentage of all parcels in each cell; row and column percentage distributions should also be developed where useful)

   Table B2b. Median Number of Fires per Parcel with Fire Damage by Census Tract (numbers = respective medians for each cell)

3. Property liens

   Table B3a. Percentage of Parcels with Any Liens by Census Tract (a threshold of liens over $100 may be advisable)

   Table B3b. Median Number of Liens Per Parcel with Any Liens by Census Tract

4. Tax arrears

   Table B4a. Percentage of Parcels with Any Tax Arrears by Census Tract

   Table B4b. Median Amount of Tax Arrears in Relation to Parcels in Arrears by Census Tract

5. Sales and median prices

   Table B5b. Median Sales Price Per Parcel for Properties Sold by Census Tract (based on the most recent sales price)

   Table B5c. Median Sales/Assessment Ratio of Sold Parcels by Census Tract

6. Dwelling count

   Table B6. Total Number of Dwelling Units by Census Tract (average number of dwellings per parcel would also be created within this table)

7. Resident ownership[1]

   Table B7. Percentage of Parcels Resident Owned by Census Tract (based on identity of owner and parcel address or Johnson Directory)

[1]New tables, not part of the A series, since they apply only to residential properties.

The following should at least be done on a sample basis:

8. Conditions[1]

Table B8. Percentage of Parcels Deteriorating by Census Tract (based on field survey)

9. More market data (Arm's-Length Transactions, A.L.T., only)[1]

Table B9a. Percentage of A.L.T. Sales of All Sales by Census Tract

Table B9b. Median A.L.T. Sales Price by Census Tract

Table B9c. Median A.L.T. Sales/Assessment Ratio by Census Tract

Table B9d. Median Length of Time on Market, A.L.T. Sales by Census Tract

Table B9e. Median Asking/Sales Price Ratios, A.L.T. Sales by Census Tract

Tables Monitoring Change

When time series data become available, the *same* third factors that emerged above as most useful are aggregated to develop the following:

Table B1. Absolute Change in Parcel Count and Land Uses by Census Tract (percentage change in count may be useful as well)

Table B2. Percentage of Change (+/−) in Number of Parcels with Fires by Census Tract

Table B3. Percentage of Change (+/−) in Number of Parcels with Liens by Census Tract

Table B4. Percentage of Change in Number of Parcels in Tax Arrears by Census Tract

Table B5. Percentage of Change (+/−) in Median Sales Prices by Census Tract

Table B6. Absolute Change (+/−) in Dwelling Count by Census Tract (percentage of change in count may be useful as well)

Table B7. Percentage of Change in Number of Resident-Owned Parcels by Census Tract

Table B8. Percentage of Change in Number of Deteriorating Parcels by Census Tract

References

City of New Haven. 1985. *Managing Municipal Information Needs Using Microcomputers: Conference Summary and Background Materials.* New Haven.

Goetze, Rolf. 1979. *Understanding Neighborhood Change: The Role of Expectations in Urban Revitalization.* Cambridge, Mass.: Ballinger.

Synnott, William R., and William H. Gruber. 1981. *Information Resource Management: Opportunities and Strategies for the 1980s.* New York: John Wiley.

4

Microcomputer Techniques for Projection and Forecasting

Mathew E. MacIver

Many of the questions asked of planners and public managers can be answered easily by referencing data that have been collected, at one point or another, as part of a field survey. A request for the location of vacant lands suited to a developer's specific needs might begin, for example, with an ordered search of the local assessor's files. Similarly, the need to know what types of new construction are occurring in different sections of the city might send the planner to the local building inspector's office to examine, sort, and summarize data collected on the job. The most compelling problems likely to be encountered here are finding the right information sources, verifying their accuracy, and applying cost-effective methods for analyzing data and presenting results. Previous chapters have shown that generic data base management software, when applied according to simple organizational principles, can easily help solve most of these inventory problems.

Sometimes, however, questions cannot be answered accurately using existing field information, either because the right data are not available or because existing data are out of date. Special field surveys can sometimes capture missing information, but the costs of designing and conducting such surveys, even using small samples, can limit the scope of study and reduce the frequency with which they can be used. In cases where surveys are not appropriate, the most suitable alternative is to extrapolate or otherwise estimate values of interest using whatever partial information may be available. Planners rely on many types of projection models for this purpose, using either older time series data or proxy variables related in some way to the missing values. The accuracy of a projection relies in large part on different sets of assumptions concerning (1) the underlying internal relationships embedded in the model itself or (2) the rates at which relevant external factors have affected the proxy variables or time series data in the past. Projection results are current only up to the day, month, or year for which assumptions have been chosen. When assumptions are chosen about how trends will change in the times to come, the projection can be used to answer questions about the future and is called a *forecast.*

The final choice of assumptions is ultimately founded on balanced, intuitive judgment, but previously hidden scenarios may come to light if the analyst can compare the effects of different assumptions or model configurations. The microcomputer offers tremendous speed advantages over other methods of performing model calculations, as long as software is available to do the job. Spreadsheet software was initially used to support business managers and analysts working with financial models in the same comparative fashion, so this type of software is also well suited to creating projections and forecasts useful to local government. Although the row and column video representation of the worksheet resembles an empty ledger book, the cells created by row and column intersections can accommodate any kind of data. This includes not just numbers but words and formulas to relate individual cell values to one another. Most of these packages also have built-in arithmetic and business functions as well as simple programing capabilities.

Spreadsheet packages can also calculate a few simple descriptive statistics, but other software is more suitable for advanced work. Many of the statistical packages that planners have used on larger time-sharing machines (such as SPSS, and SAS) have now been downsized to fit smaller systems. The Lincoln Institute's SOLIR software, designed exclusively for microcomputer hardware, combines descriptive, associative, and inferential statistical routines with a data base management program and a modest geoprocessing module. The analysis of tabular data with spatial meaning is greatly facilitated by the thematic mapping capability offered by the latter module.

Inexpensive microcomputer hardware, combined with powerful generic software, has increased the analytic options available to staff responsible for projection and forecasting studies. Many techniques that relied heavily on sheer computational power can now be accommodated on desktop machines. Less mathematically demanding procedures (such as descriptive statistical measures or frequency distributions) can be used more often as well, increasing the time available for exploring alternative modeling assumptions. As a result, much more attention can be devoted to assessing the comparative merits of different analytical procedures. Assessment criteria include the following:

- *The quality of the results* that each family of model is theoretically and practically capable of producing. The quality of a model's results depends on the theoretical underpinnings of the model structure, the reasonableness of its assumptions, the quality of the data, and the skill of the model builder.

• *The probable costs* attached to each modeling alternative. Costs include the expense of capturing data, the amount of staff time needed to perform the analysis, and the costs of computer hardware and software.

• *The implementation time and accuracy tolerances* required by those who use the model results. Projection and forecasting models are assumed to be used most often to support decisions taken at management and policy levels in local government. Models can be used for creating benchmark projections and forecasts for continued use across many different types of local government planning activities or for special one-off ad hoc studies of the impacts that certain decisions may have on local service levels, operating and capital budgets, local economic activity, or other issues of interest other than sensitive issues. Here a great premium is placed on timeliness of the analytic response and an honest assessment of model accuracy.

The following sections will show how the use of microcomputers can influence decisions on modeling techniques according to each of the above categories. Three families of models will be discussed. We will begin by examining aggregate trending techniques and then move to component (or accounting) models that use disaggregated data to trace changes in local populations and economies. Finally, we will look at more advanced linear methods that may be of occasional help to local government planners. Examples used to illustrate these techniques may be helpful in their own right; the techniques can be easily adapted to slightly different software packages and locally available data.

Aggregate Trending Models

The concept underlying aggregate trending techniques is disarmingly simple: variables change in perceptible and regular ways over time. Time is a proxy independent variable that represents all the factors that may have influenced the growth or decline of the chosen dependent variable. When simple time series information is plotted on an *X/Y* graph, the shape of the line that is produced when the dots are connected usually conforms best to one type of additive, multiplicative, or logarithmic function. (Figure 4.1 shows several curves both graphically and mathematically.) The equation can then be applied to fill in the gaps between past observations or to extrapolate future variable values.

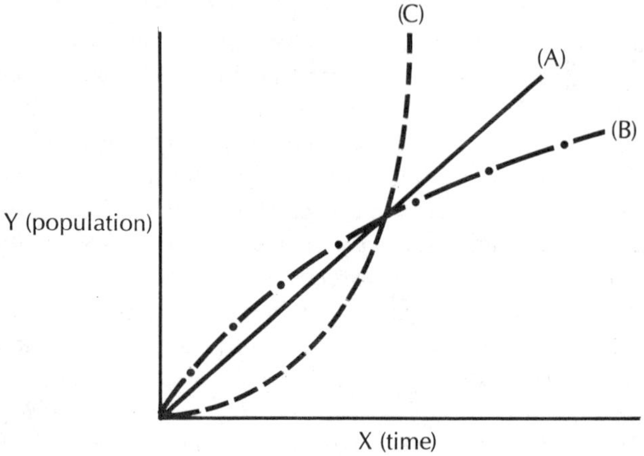

(A): Linear Function: $Y = a + b X$, where $a = 0, b > 1$
(B): Power Function: $\log Y = \log a + b \log X$, where $0 < b < 1$
(C): Exponential Function: $\log Y = \log a + X \log b$, where $a, b, X > 0$

Figure 4.1. *Sample trending curves.*

Although time elapses at a constant rate, the effects of time as a variable in a linear equation are by no means equally constant. The mix of factors that influence a variable over time may certainly change, as may the intensity with which individual hidden independent variables (comprising the time proxy) exercise influence over the dependent term. There is also the question of an appropriate time frame; curves can change shape dramatically depending on the slice of the past used to project the future. Trends projected from data drawn over a longer time period will smooth short-term anomalies but will also include changes that might have occurred in an entirely different set of circumstances. Conversely, smaller windows into past trends may also lend inappropriately greater weight to short-term phenomena.

Trending models alone cannot answer questions about which implicit factors may be more or less important or about whether any one time frame will be satisfactory for the specific purposes of the projection. An aggregate trend model is theory-neutral; the calculation only describes a line between a series of independent observations and does not explain or justify the links between the many constituent events or trends that influence each observation. The aggregate trend model is simply a mathematical representation of the analyst's judgment concerning which determinants of change have had the greatest influence on the value of a gross observation as well as how these factors might change over time. The analyst then fits an appropriate curve to the set of observations that corresponds most closely to the assumptions he has chosen.

Local jurisdictions often use aggregate trending population projection techniques to guide many incremental decisions concerning the distribution of government resources. Some decisions must be based on an estimate of the absolute number of people living in a particular district, but many more policy level decisions require only an estimate of the proportion of residents living in an area, compared to the total number of residents in a jurisdiction. If a highly accurate head count is not necessary or feasible in the period between census surveys, simple trending calculations can provide inexpensive estimates of tract or block populations, particularly in the first few years after the census has been conducted. The accuracy of such extrapolations cannot be tested, however, so trends drawn for areas showing obvious changes in rates of growth or decline must be carefully and explicitly qualified.

The example in Table 4.1 shows a microcomputer implementation of two related population trending models applied to the twenty-seven census tracts in Leon County, Florida (Sipe and Hopkins 1984). The linear trending model simply assumes that the average annual population increase between 1970 and 1980 will remain constant over the desired projection period. Once this annual increase is calculated, it is multiplied by the number of years in the projection and added to the base period population—in this case, the 1980 census figures. The resulting curve, therefore, is a straight line. The second model assumes that the rate of growth over the prior ten-year period will remain constant and, using natural logarithms, applies this rate over the specified projection period. This yields a curve described by an exponential function.

If the analyst believes that some tracts will experience constant rates of growth in the future, the exponential model may be appropriate. The exponential model will also dampen the effect of radical population decline so that zero or negative population estimates—a very rare condition in the real world—cannot be produced. On the other hand, exponential growth rates are sustainable only until *build-out* occurs, or until the supply of public services can catch up with demand. This, of course, cannot be represented directly in the exponential function used to derive the projection, although it could be represented in a function with discrete limits (such as logistic functions or Gompertz curves). The choice of an appropriate model rests entirely on situational analysis rather than meaningful explanatory measures of fit.

What are the advantages of the aggregate trending approach? Cost is a compelling factor. Census information is readily available, and the skills needed to calculate the projections are minimal. The spreadsheet

Table 4.1
Population Projection Template: Linear and Exponential

Census Tract	*Census Tract Population*		*1990 Census Tract Population Projection*		
	1970	*1980*	*Linear*	*Exponential*	
1	1,077	513	0	−0.74	244
2	4,106	4,007	3,908	−0.02	3,910
3	3,946	5,204	6,462	0.28	6,863
4	3,373	2,583	1,793	−0.27	1,978
5	3,371	2,630	1,889	−0.25	2,052
6	4,304	3,847	3,390	−0.11	3,439
7	2,388	2,142	1,896	−0.11	1,921
8	2,387	2,632	2,877	0.10	2,902
9	5,249	7,460	9,671	0.35	10,602
10	3,912	4,764	5,616	0.20	5,802
11	4,626	5,301	5,976	0.14	6,074
12	1,982	1,299	616	−0.42	851
13	4,306	4,273	4,240	−0.01	4,240
14	4,380	6,070	7,760	0.33	8,412
15	3,301	3,448	3,595	0.04	3,602
16	3,034	5,566	8,098	0.61	10,211
17	4,057	6,043	8,029	0.40	9,001
18	3,625	5,445	7,265	0.41	8,179
19	6,557	7,306	8,055	0.11	8,141
20	7,921	10,226	12,531	0.26	13,202
21	3,835	9,151	14,467	0.87	21,836
22	4,278	8,222	12,166	0.65	15,802
23	2,078	5,747	9,416	1.02	15,894
24	3,217	12,853	22,489	1.39	51,352
25	6,380	11,080	15,780	0.55	19,242
26	2,748	5,502	8,256	0.69	11,016
27	2,606	5,341	8,076	0.72	10,946

1970 county population	103,407
1980 county population	148,665
Projected population	190,100
Projection year	1990

Adapted from Sipe and Hopkins (1984).

program required only a few minutes of data entry time, including the time needed to place each simple equation into the appropriate cell. Because the program allows the operator to replicate the contents of one cell across all others using the same calculation, the equations needed to be entered only once. After two or three days of practice, creating a spreadsheet such as the one in Table 4.1 takes only one or two hours.

The greatest expense in aggregate trending will accrue to the head-ware needed to ensure that acceptable accuracy tolerances have been achieved. If a relatively higher level of accuracy is needed, other data such as building permits, auto registrations, school enrollments, or vital statistics can be used to cross-check results. The decision to collect and integrate these supplementary indicators of change with raw projection results depends on the confidence of the analyst, the time and money available to track down supporting records, and the degree of accuracy demanded of the projection. Again, this is a question of judgment.

Component Models

Sometimes planners need techniques that allocate the results of trends measured more exactly over a broader population. Sometimes it is desirable to split larger trends into components that give the analyst a better feeling for the sources of community change. These so-called component models either divide larger trends into more manageable pieces or use individual components of change to create more precise aggregated projections. We will continue to use the population example above to demonstrate the principles, costs, and benefits involved with both approaches but will also explore the use of one component technique for basic economic analysis.

Population Component Analysis

Most county and state governments make population projections at the county level using component methods that are based on more current data than are available to local jurisdictions. The projections are rarely extrapolated to local governments, however, because of the time and expense that these different models require. But local jurisdictions can easily disaggregate county or state results into pieces that correspond to smaller geographical areas, such as census tracts, political districts, or other enumeration areas where time series information is available for a period that corresponds to the more accurate county estimates.

The first method calculates the percentage of growth that each of many smaller constituent districts contributed to a larger enumeration area (usually the county) over a discrete time period, usually census years. Each percentage is thereafter presumed to remain constant and is applied to projected county populations for following years. This is the share method of component disaggregation. The shift method, by contrast, compares the shares of the larger area that each district held in two different periods and adds the (positive or negative) change in percentage to the percentage share of the last period. This trended percentage is then applied to the county total. Table 4.2 shows the

Table 4.2
Population Projection Template: Share and Shift

Census Tract	*Census Tract Population*		*1990 Census Tract Population Projection*	
	1970	*1980*	*Share*	*Shift*
1	1,077	513	0	0
2	4,106	4,007	3,916	2,699
3	3,946	5,204	6,356	6,055
4	3,373	2,583	1,860	405
5	3,371	2,630	1,952	529
6	4,304	3,847	3,429	1,926
7	2,388	2,142	1,917	1,088
8	2,387	2,632	2,856	2,343
9	5,249	7,460	9,484	9,429
10	3,912	4,764	5,544	4,992
11	4,626	5,301	5,919	5,053
12	1,982	1,299	674	0
13	4,306	4,273	4,243	3,012
14	4,380	6,070	7,617	7,472
15	3,301	3,448	3,583	2,750
16	3,034	5,566	7,884	8,657
17	4,057	6,043	7,861	7,996
18	3,625	5,445	7,111	7,261
19	6,557	7,306	7,992	6,630
20	7,921	10,226	12,336	11,591
21	3,835	9,151	14,018	16,353
22	4,278	8,222	11,833	13,163
23	2,078	5,747	9,106	10,877
24	3,217	12,853	21,675	26,957
25	6,380	11,080	15,383	16,608
26	2,748	5,502	8,023	9,019
27	2,606	5,341	7,845	8,868

1970 county population	103,407
1980 county population	148,665
Projected population	190,100
Projection year	1990

Adapted from Sipe and Hopkins (1984).

application of both methods to the Leon County data used above. Note that the structure of the spreadsheet does not change at all; all that has changed are the underlying formulas used in the spreadsheet columns that contain the projections for each of the new methods.

Obviously, there is still the problem of assuming that trends in the percentage allocations of county growth will be distributed in the same manner as they were in previous years. This assumption is subject to the same misgivings expressed in the discussion of aggregate trending techniques. What are the advantages, then, to these approaches? The individual projections are, in total, constrained by the larger county forecast. The sources of potential error in the bigger jurisdiction are likely to be better defined, and when split across a large number of smaller districts, the effects of the modeling error attributable to the county forecasting technique are diffused as well. If the reverse process were used—or individual district estimates were totaled to the county level—the effects of the less detectable measurement errors in the smaller areas will be totaled as well.

Why use these techniques at all, though, if state- and county-level forecasting methods can be applied at the local level? Agencies in larger jurisdictions usually use the cohort survival method, another form of component analysis, to project future population levels. With this technique, a county population is divided into cohorts, such as five-year age groups stratified by sex. Each cohort has its own survival rate over a five-year span, and the first (age 0 to 4) cohort is replenished by a birth rate applied to the female cohorts of child-bearing age. After each five-year cycle, populations in each cohort are reduced in proportion to the appropriate survival rate and advance to the next five-year age group. Birth and death rates can be obtained from local sources of vital statistics.

If all communities were sealed in a way that prevented movement among them, the model might be more readily usable for smaller areas (though its assumption of constant birth rates clearly carries liabilities). But in- and out-migration rates significantly affect the growth or decline of many cohorts and so figure prominently in determining the accuracy of the projection. Net migration rates are very difficult to calculate from spot field checks in small areas, but state governments have a variety of methods to trace the numbers of those who come and go from county-level jurisdictions. The most important source of migration rate data is the revenue office, which annually processes detailed tax information. This information is not broadly available to local jurisdictions in forms that can be used with confidence in such aggregational models. Because there are fewer counties, however, the expense of aggregating records to many fewer, larger geographical entities is much less. The results can be split among many constituent local government areas that then have only to worry about their own micro net migration rates or severe age or sex anomalies (such as large military installations, universities, and retirement populations).

Table 4.3 shows an example of a cohort survival model implemented with the same spreadsheeet software that was used to create our other component models. In this application, each age cohort is allocated one line in the worksheet, divided by sex, with death and net migration

Table 4.3
Population Component Model II, Cohort Survival

Net Migration	*Death Rate*	*Male*	*Age*	*Female*	*Death Rate*	*Net Migration*	*Birth Rate*
	.00	5,000	0–4	5,000	.00		
	0.01	4,995	5–9	4,995	0.01		
	0.01	4,970	10–14	4,970	0.01		
0.01	0.02	4,935	15–19	4,935	0.02	0.01	0.25
0.01	0.02	4,836	20–24	4,837	0.02	0.01	0.35
0.02	0.03	4,739	25–29	4,740	0.03	0.02	0.45
0.02	0.03	4,597	30–34	4,598	0.03	0.02	0.70
0.03	0.03	4,459	35–39	4,460	0.03	0.03	0.45
0.03	0.03	4,325	40–44	4,326	0.03	0.03	0.25
0.02	0.03	4,195	45–49	4,196	0.03	0.02	
0.01	0.04	4,069	50–54	4,070	0.04	0.01	
−0.01	0.05	3,906	55–59	3,907	0.05	−0.01	
−0.02	0.06	3,711	60–64	3,712	0.06	−0.02	
−0.03	0.10	3,488	65–69	3,489	0.08	−0.03	
−0.02	0.15	3,136	70–74	3,210	0.10	−0.02	
−0.01	0.20	2,728	75–79	2,889	0.15	−0.01	
0.00	0.25	2,310	80–84	2,450	0.20	0.00	
0.00	0.50	1,733	85–89	1,960	0.50	0.00	
0.00	0.80	866	90–94	980	0.80	0.00	
0.00		173	95–99	196		0.00	

rates applied differentially to each age or sex grouping. In addition, net fertility rates are shown for female cohorts of child-bearing age. In the United States there will be little need to use different net migration rates between sexes, but in many less developed countries there may be marked gender-based migration rate differences in cohorts above age 15. Death rates also differ between men and women in most communities. This spreadsheet could also be combined with one that showed the consequences of alternative projections on gross population totals over as many five-year periods as desired.

Although this component model can trace the ebb and flow of populations across larger areas, the mathematics do not tell us whether or not our assumptions are correct. Migration assumptions are the most "iffy" and must often be subjectively chosen from intelligence gathered from other sources. Because the economic vitality of a town or region is often the major determinant of future migration movement, the analyst must search for data and methods that help to indicate which sectors of an economy are changing most radically and which will have the greatest impact on employment and local consumption.

Economic Component Models

County and national economic data are widely available in a disaggregated form that is extremely useful for tracing the employment effects of industrial growth and decline. Economic base methods used to perform this type of analysis are easily accommodated in a spreadsheet format as well.

Basic economic theory posits that economic output in urban areas can be divided into one portion that serves local consumption requirements (nonbasic production) and another portion that is exported to destinations outside of the jurisdiction's immediate economic frontier (basic production). In a simple accounting sense, local economics expand over a discrete period at a rate proportional to the ratio between basic and nonbasic output, net of goods and services imported for local consumption. The accounting framework is logical but theoretically fragile in the sense that it does not automatically account for differences in nonbasic output per unit of basic output between different types of industry. (However, individual basic employment multipliers can be calculated for different industry classifications, if time and resources permit.) Agglomeration economies, or feedback effects between different industries, cannot be isolated easily. Measurement problems are also rife; employment is usually used as a proxy measurement for output measures, yet each industry uses different mixes of labor and capital to achieve identical production levels. Finally, it is difficult to distinguish which portions of an industry's output are actually basic or nonbasic, even without concerning ourselves with the geographical imprecisions implicit in defining a jurisdiction's economic boundaries.

Despite these difficulties, smaller jurisdictions can rarely afford to use more elaborate and precise alternatives, such as input/output analysis techniques. Defining potentially upcoming or lagging economic sectors with the precision that other methods can provide may not, in fact, be needed if all that is required is a broad-brush analysis of local economic trends. The turnaround time for creating basic and nonbasic models to help local leaders understand gross economic trends is also relatively short when relationships are constructed using generic spreadsheet software.

Figure 4.2a illustrates one technique for dividing local employment into basic and nonbasic categories. This model compares the share of employment that each sector of the local economy contributes to total local (in this case, county) employment, in comparison to analogous sectoral shares at the national level. The differences in share percentages between national and local sectors are then multiplied by local employ-

	A	C	D	F	H	J	L	N
80								
81	====	====	====	====	====	====	====	====
82	CALCULATION OF LOCATION QUOTIENTS							
83							EMPLOYMENT	
84	SIC		UNITED STATES		LOCAL GOVERNMENT		FOR LOCAL	EXPORT
85	CODE	DESCRIPTION	EMPLOYMENT	% OF TOTAL	EMPLOYMENT	% OF TOTAL	REQUIREMENT	EMPLOYMENT
86	----	----	----	----	----	----	----	----
87		CONTRACT CONSTRUCTION						
88		----						
89	15	GENERAL CONTRACTORS	1173000	1.30%	940	2.57%	475	465
90	16	HEAVY CONSTRUCTION	926900	1.03%	491	1.34%	375	116
91	17	SPECIAL TRADE	2246200	2.48%	2148	5.87%	909	1239
92	--	ALL OTHERS						
93								
94		MANUFACTURING						
95		----						
96	20	FOOD AND KINDRED PRODUCTS	1708000	1.89%	158	0.43%	691	0
97	24	LUMBER AND WOOD PRODUCTS	690500	0.76%	384	1.05%	279	105
98	27	PRINTING AND PUBLISHING	1252100	1.38%	437	1.19%	507	0
99	32	STONE, CLAY AND GLASS	662100	0.73%	183	0.50%	268	0
100	35	MACHINERY EXCEPT ELECTRICAL	2494000	2.76%	385	1.05%	1009	0
101	38	INSTRUMENTS AND RELATED PRODUCTS	711300	0.79%	54	0.15%	288	0
102	--	ALL OTHERS	12767000	14.12%	2567	7.02%	5166	0
103								
104		TRANSPORTATION & PUBLIC UTILITIES						
105		----						
106	42	TRUCKING AND WAREHOUSING	1280200	1.42%	179	0.49%	518	0
107	47	TRANSPORTATION SERVICES	197600	0.22%	59	0.16%	80	0
108	49	ELECTRIC, GAS & SANITARY SERVICES	827400	0.92%	211	0.58%	335	0
109	--	ALL OTHERS	2840800	3.14%	1041	2.85%	1150	0
110								
111		WHOLESALE TRADE						
112		----						
113	50	WHOLESALE TRADE - DURABLES	3122000	3.45%	948	2.59%	1263	0
114	51	WHOLESALE TRADE - NONDURABLES	2153000	2.38%	718	1.96%	871	0
115	--	ALL OTHERS	0	0.00%	0	0.00%	0	0
116								
117		RETAIL TRADE						
118		----						
119	53	GENERAL MERCHANDISE	2244600	2.48%	1494	4.08%	908	586
120	54	FOOD STORES	2383600	2.64%	1787	4.88%	965	822
121	55	AUTO DEALERS & SERVICE STATIONS	1688500	1.87%	1222	3.34%	683	539
122	56	APPAREL AND ACCESSORY STORES	956700	1.06%	734	2.01%	387	347
123	57	FURNITURE AND HOME FURNISHINGS	606400	0.67%	496	1.36%	245	251
124	58	EATING AND DRINKING PLACES	4625800	5.12%	4282	11.70%	1872	2410
125	59	MISCELLANEOUS RETAIL	1912200	2.12%	1411	3.86%	774	637
126	--	ALL OTHERS	617400	0.68%	493	1.35%	250	243
127								
128		FINANCE, INSURANCE & REAL ESTATE						
129		----						
130	60	BANKING	1570600	1.74%	654	1.79%	636	18
131	61	CREDIT AGENCIES OTHER THAN BANKS	569800	0.63%	340	0.93%	231	109
132	63	INSURANCE CARRIERS	1224100	1.35%	1387	3.79%	495	892
133	65	REAL ESTATE	981000	1.09%	734	2.01%	397	337
134	--	ALL OTHERS	700200	0.77%	272	0.74%	283	0
135								
136		SERVICES						
137		----						
138	70	HOTELS AND OTHER LODGING	1075800	1.19%	751	2.05%	435	316
139	72	PERSONAL SERVICES	900700	1.00%	598	1.63%	364	234
140	73	BUSINESS SERVICES	3092000	3.42%	1040	2.84%	1251	0
141	75	AUTO REPAIR, SERVICES & GARAGES	570900	0.63%	362	0.99%	231	131
142	76	MISCELLANEOUS REPAIR	288800	0.32%	186	0.51%	117	69
143	78	MOTION PICTURES	216900	0.24%	104	0.28%	88	16
144	79	AMUSEMENT & RECREATION	763500	0.84%	278	0.76%	309	0
145	80	HEALTH SERVICES	4295900	4.75%	3071	8.39%	1738	1333
146	81	LEGAL SERVICES	497700	0.55%	373	1.02%	201	172
147	82	EDUCATION SERVICES	1138200	1.26%	270	0.74%	461	0
148	83	SOCIAL SERVICES	1134300	1.25%	694	1.90%	459	235
149	86	MEMBERSHIP ORGANIZATIONS	1539300	1.70%	635	1.74%	623	12
150	89	MISCELLANEOUS SERVICES	997400	1.10%	1114	3.05%	404	710
151	--	ALL OTHERS	35000	0.04%	20	0.05%	14	6
152								
153								
154		OTHERS:						
155	--	NONCLASSIFIABLE ESTABLISHMENTS	18727000	20.71%	878	2.40%	7578	0
156								
157		TOTAL	90406400	100.00%	36583	100.00%		12350
158								

Figure 4.2a. *Sample template.*

	A	B	C	D	E	F	G	H	I	J	K	L	M	N
80														
81	==													
82	CALCULATIONS OF EMPLOYMENT SHIFT/SHARES													
83														
84					UNITED STATES				LOCAL GOVERNMENT					
85	SIC			EMPLOYMENT				EMPLOYMENT			NATIONAL	INDUSTRIAL	COMPETITIVE	TOTAL
86	CODE		DESCRIPTION	1977	1980		% CHANGE	1977	1980	% CHANGE	GROWTH	MIX	SHARE	CHANGE
87	-----		---------------------	------	------		------	------	------	------	------	------	------	------
88			.CONTRACT CONSTRUCTION											
89			---------------------											
90	15		GENERAL CONTRACTORS	1108400	1173000		5.83%	874	940	7.55%	84	-33	15	66
91	16		HEAVY CONSTRUCTION	787100	926900		17.76%	303	491	62.05%	29	25	134	188
92	17		SPECIAL TRADE	1955300	2246200		14.88%	1460	2148	47.12%	140	77	471	688
93	--		ALL OTHERS	0	0		0.00%	0	0	0.00%	0	0	0	0
94														
95			MANUFACTURING											
96			---------------------											
97	20		FOOD AND KINDRED PROD.	1711000	1708000		-0.18%	647	158	-75.58%	62	-63	-488	-489
98	24		LUMBER AND WOOD PROD.	721900	690500		-4.35%	487	384	-21.15%	47	-68	-82	-103
99	27		PRINTING AND PUBLISHING	1141400	1252100		9.70%	357	437	22.41%	34	0	45	80
100	32		STONE, CLAY & GLASS	668700	662100		-0.99%	178	183	2.81%	17	-19	7	5
101	35		MACHINERY EXCEPT ELEC.	2174700	2494000		14.68%	300	385	28.33%	29	15	41	85
102	38		INSTRUMENTS	615100	711300		15.64%	0	54	0.00%	0	0	0	54
103	--		ALL OTHERS	12649200	12767000		0.93%	2167	2567	18.46%	209	-188	380	400
104														
105			TRANSPORTATION											
106			---------------------											
107	42		TRUCKING & WAREHOUSING	1219500	1280200		4.98%	164	179	9.15%	16	-8	7	15
108	47		TRANSPORTATION SERVICES	155500	197600		27.07%	0	59	0.00%	0	0	0	59
109	49		ELECTRIC, GAS, SANITARY	745700	827400		10.96%	107	211	97.20%	10	1	92	104
110	--		ALL OTHERS	2592300	2840800		9.59%	1024	1041	1.66%	99	0	-81	17
111														
112			WHOLESALE TRADE											
113			--------------------											
114	50		WHOLESALE-DURABLES	2717000	3122000		14.91%	831	948	14.08%	80	44	-7	117
115	51		WHOLESALE-NONDURABLES	1991000	2153000		8.14%	694	718	3.46%	67	-10	-32	24
116	--		ALL OTHERS	0	0		0.00%	0	0	0.00%	0	0	0	0
117														
118			RETAIL TRADE											
119			-------------------											
120	53		GENERAL MERCHANDISE	2204300	2244600		1.83%	1130	1494	32.21%	109	-88	343	364
121	54		FOOD STORES	2106300	2383600		13.17%	1593	1787	12.18%	153	56	-16	194
122	55		AUTO DEALERS	1800800	1688500		-6.24%	1355	1222	-9.82%	130	-215	-49	-133
123	56		APPAREL AND ACCESSORIES	869900	956700		9.98%	582	734	26.12%	56	2	94	152
124	57		FURNITURE & FURNISHINGS	562500	606400		7.80%	377	496	31.56%	36	-7	90	119
125	58		EATING AND DRINKING	3948600	4625800		17.15%	2858	4282	49.83%	275	215	934	1424
126	59		MISCELLANEOUS RETAIL	1739700	1912200		9.92%	1120	1411	25.98%	108	3	180	291
127	--		ALL OTHERS	575800	617400		7.22%	315	493	56.51%	30	-8	155	178
128														
129			FINANCE, INSURANCE, REAL ESTATE											
130			----------------------											
131	60		BANKING	1356700	1570600		15.77%	555	654	17.84%	53	34	11	99
132	61		CREDIT AGENCIES	477700	569800		19.28%	310	340	9.68%	30	30	-30	30
133	63		INSURANCE CARRIERS	1140900	1224100		7.29%	710	1387	95.35%	68	-17	625	677
134	65		REAL ESTATE	815000	981000		20.37%	765	734	-4.05%	74	82	-187	-31
135	--		ALL OTHERS	676700	700200		3.47%	330	272	-17.58%	32	-20	-69	-58
136														
137			SERVICES											
138			-------------------											
139	70		HOTELS AND LODGING	956100	1075800		12.52%	540	751	39.07%	52	16	143	211
140	72		PERSONAL SERVICES	888100	900700		1.42%	515	598	16.12%	50	-42	76	83
141	73		BUSINESS SERVICES	2357200	3092000		31.17%	629	1040	65.34%	61	136	215	411
142	75		AUTO REPAIR	497700	570900		14.71%	254	362	42.52%	24	13	71	108
143	76		MISCELLANEOUS REPAIR	240700	288800		19.98%	124	186	50.00%	12	13	37	62
144	78		MOTION PICTURES	214000	216900		1.36%	70	104	48.57%	7	-6	33	34
145	79		AMUSEMENT & RECREATION	665700	763500		14.69%	197	278	41.12%	19	10	52	81
146	80		HEALTH SERVICES	4583900	4295900		-6.28%	1599	3071	92.06%	154	-254	1572	1472
147	81		LEGAL SERVICES	393900	497700		26.35%	280	373	33.21%	27	47	19	93
148	82		EDUCATION SERVICES	1031000	1138200		10.40%	290	270	-6.90%	28	2	-50	-20
149	83		SOCIAL SERVICES	854600	1134300		32.73%	380	694	82.63%	37	88	190	314
150	86		MEMBERSHIP ORGAN.	1495400	1539300		2.94%	461	635	37.74%	44	-31	160	174
151	89		MISCELLANEOUS SERVICES	786800	997400		26.77%	763	1114	46.00%	73	131	147	351
152	--		ALL OTHERS	0	35000		0.00%	0	20	0.00%	0	0	0	20
153														
154			OTHERS											
155			---------------------											
156	--		NONCLASSIFIABLE ESTAB	16277200	18727000		15.05%	97	878	805.15%	9	5	766	781
157														
158			<<<<TOTALS>>>>	82471000	90406400		9.62%	27792	36583	31.63%	2674	-32	6016	8791

Figure 4.2b. *Sample template.*

ment totals in each category. These jobs are classified as those that contribute to export-oriented, or basic, economic activity. Nonbasic employment can then be calculated by simply subtracting export employment from total employment. The ratio of basic to nonbasic jobs can then be used as a multiplier to estimate the total employment impact deriving from added or subtracted increments or decrements to basic employment levels. Figure 4.2b shows an elaboration of the technique, further disaggregating trends in overall local employment into components attributable to changes in total national employment, changes in the mix of employment across different industrial sectors, and changes within the same industry at both national and local levels. Employment shifts are all easily calculated using only national and local employment totals, by sector, over a two-period time series.

The model is flawed in many respects. It assumes that the disaggregated export component is, in fact, successfully absorbed by the nation as a whole, without taking into account the many transaction costs or potentially weakening national markets that may prevent product diffusion—and income infusion—from occurring. Employment indicators also cannot be used to estimate outward capital flows; negative employment figures make no sense. Still, the model can be used to direct attention to broad sectoral strengths and weaknesses in a local economy. Furthermore, the analysis produces a multiplicative term that can at least partially indicate the magnitude of total employment returns that can be expected per unit of additional investment in specific industries. When combined with detailed intuitive knowledge of local resources, these estimates can be used in conjunction with other population, land use, and budgetary projection procedures. Finally, the analysis can always be improved by using additional time series information to uncover continuing trends and, most significant, exceptions to trends that signal either crisis or opportunity.

The spreadsheet matrix is ideally suited to component analysis for both population and economic base studies. The procedures described here demand little data beyond those commonly available from ongoing government reporting programs; the time and out-of-pocket costs needed to structure the models and key enter data are minimal. This approach presents tremendous advantages to analysts operating under severe budgetary and time constraints, but we have also demonstrated that the theoretical underpinnings of these very accessible models can be questioned from various points of view. If assumptions and findings are appropriately qualified, however, even relatively small benefits can justify the inconsiderable expense incurred by microcomputer-based approaches.

Linear Regression Techniques

Chapter 3 described the use of simple two-way frequency distributions to uncover associative relationships between different indicators of neighborhood change. Tables that are "nested" within each other allow analysts to perceive slight changes in neighborhood conditions that may be interrelated. The chi-squared test can be used for matrix models of this type to estimate the probability that such relationships may have occurred by chance, and correlation analysis can measure the strength of linear relationships. The use of results from these tests is limited, though, in that they cannot provide information about whether changes in one variable might partially cause changes in another; moreover, the results of associative tests are not particularly suitable for application to hypothetical situations. Linear regression models, on the other hand, show the respective contributions of several variables to a given outcome and trace the effects that changes in one variable may have on another, providing analysts with a tool for exploring the consequences of change. Although all introductory statistical textbooks treat linear regression in greater depth than is possible here, we should review the technique before showing how it can be applied through microcomputer software.

A linear model posits that for every change in an *independent* variable X, a corresponding change occurs in the value of the *dependent* variable Y. When the analyst plots observed X,Y values on a grid, creating a scattergram, the magnitude and direction of the change can be roughly estimated by eye. To obtain an estimate of greater precision, however, a line of the form

$$Y = a + bX$$

can be fitted to the observations, yielding a constant value a that marks the point where the line hits the Y axis of the grid (the *intercept*), and a constant value b that indicates the *slope* of the line. The latter term shows how much the dependent variable Y changes in relationship to the independent variable X. Although there are many lines that could be drawn through a scattergram, there is only one that minimizes the total sum of the distances between the observed Y (Y_o) values and the estimated values of Y (Y_e) on the specified line. This minimizing procedure, called the ordinary least squares method, is preferred to other alternatives because it is statistically unbiased and shows less variance than other linear estimators.

There are several ways to determine the quality of a linear model specification. First, it is determined in part by the magnitude of the sum of the squared differences between observed and predicted Y values.

This is called the standard error of estimate (SEE) and is analogous to the standard deviation of a population sample. The lower the SEE is in relation to the mean of *Y*, the greater the clustering of the observations. Second, the correlation coefficient *R* provides an estimate of the probability that the regression results could have occurred by chance, using a test of significance similar to the chi-squared test. Finally, the square of the correlation coefficient (R^2), or coeffecient of determination (COD), is simply the amount of the variation in *Y* that can be explained by the linear relationship, in proportion to the total variation in *Y*. A value of 1 indicates total (theoretical) explanatory value, whereas a value of 0 indicates that the model has no explanatory value.

Simple bivariate regression—that is, a regression that uses only one independent variable—can be tremendously useful for quickly exploring the consequences of different decisions. What must be avoided, however, is the temptation to specify such a model when the complexity of the relationship obviously exceeds the explanatory power of one simple determinant. Because urban systems are wonderfully complicated, this general rule of thumb might limit the number of opportunities for using simple regression methods. Even in situations where the explanatory power of the model is admittedly limited, results can be used to at least partially indicate the probable magnitude or direction of change. Moreover, the costs involved with implementing simple regression formulations using generic software are very small now, discounting data collection costs.

The Incentive Zoning Case

One good example of a quick bivariate linear regression application is provided by a study of the impacts that New York City's incentive zoning scheme had on the office market tax base there between the years 1966 and 1973 (Kayden 1978). During this period, by easing zoning regulations, the city allowed over 10 million square feet of bonus office space to be added to existing inventories in an effort to induce developers to add public amenities (such as plazas, theaters, and so forth) to their projects or to conform to alternative zoning or administrative stipulations. What was the true cost of these incentives to the city, in terms of forgone tax revenue? The question can be framed after assuming that:

Bonus office space would not have been created in the absence of incentives.

Changes in real property assessments reflect the true state of the city's real property market and not changes in the way that methodologies are applied.

Changes in vacancy rates affect real property assessments for office structures because discounted cash flow models are used to estimate office building value.

Under these assumptions, we can estimate the net change in tax revenue by specifying the relationship between actual vacancy rates and assessed valuation levels and applying the resulting model to a hypothetical market in which none of the incentive space is available. By subtracting bonus space from the total office inventory, we can calculate new vacancy rates for use as independent variables in our model. Projected assessment levels can then be multiplied by the amount of office space (net of bonus area) to calculate a new estimate of tax revenues that would have accrued to the city in a market without incentive zoning office space. A comparison of the with and without revenue projections shows how much the city has gained or lost as a result of the incentive zoning ordinance.

Table 4.4 shows an adaptation of the model used in Kayden's analysis, implemented using spreadsheet software on a typical desktop microcomputer. The first two sections of the sheet define the facts of the case for use in the regression calculations in the section below. Sums of the squared deviations for each variable are listed below the cells that contain their averages, and the specifications of the equation itself are summarized at the bottom of the section. All of the calculations here, including the *goodness of fit* measures—the correlation coefficient R and coefficient of determination (COD) R^2—are performed within the spreadsheet itself. Note that the COD approaches a value of 1; this is a very strong (almost too strong) indicator of explanatory power, especially for a simple bivariate model in which only one independent variable is fitted to the dependent term. The last section shows the comparison between revenue streams, including the net present value (NPV) of the difference between the streams. The NPV function is built into most spreadsheet packages so that the user does not need to set up procedures to build the measurement from scratch.

The NPV calculated for this adaptation of the New York case shows that, *ceteris paribus,* the city extracted a negative net benefit from the zoning ordinance. Kayden's study uses more precise data and estimates that the negative benefit was even greater. Obviously, this type of study—quickly set up and quickly executed—can offer tremendous advantages for development negotiations, legislative reviews, and executive action. The study yields an approximation of value that can be assigned, at least in part, to the consequences of a government program that either might have appeared costless or could not otherwise have been evaluated in fiscal terms. Although the precision of the estimate may be subject

Table 4.4
Costs and Benefits of Incentive Zoning

	1965	*1966*	*1967*	*1968*	*1969*	*1970*	*1971*	*1972*	*1973*
Office space (1,000 square feet)									
Total space with incentive zoning	150,000	152,000	153,500	160,000	172,500	180,500	195,500	212,500	518,500
Total space without incentive zoning	149,500	151,000	152,500	158,500	168,500	175,000	187,500	202,000	207,500
Net bonus space	500	1,000	1,000	1,500	4,000	5,500	8,000	10,500	11,000
Total occupied space (demand)	146,500	150,500	153,000	159,000	170,500	173,500	182,000	193,000	194,500
Vacancy, valuation, and tax information									
Vacancy rate with incentive zoning (*x*)	0.023	0.010	0.003	0.006	0.012	0.039	0.069	0.092	0.110
Average valuation per square foot with incentive zoning (*y*)	24.00	24.50	25.00	25.00	25.50	24.50	23.75	22.50	22.00
Vacancy rate without incentive zoning	0.020	0.003	−0.003	−0.003	−0.012	0.009	0.029	0.045	0.063
Hypothesized average valuation per square foot without incentive zoning	24.64	25.10	25.28	25.28	25.52	24.96	24.39	23.97	23.47
Tax rate	0.05	0.05	0.05	0.05	0.05	0.06	0.06	0.06	0.07
Regression calculations									
y avg (ym) = 24.08									
x avg (xm) = 0.04									
Sum $(y - ym)^2$ = 11.00	0.0064	0.1764	0.8464	0.8464	2.0164	0.1764	0.1089	2.4964	4.3264
Sum $(x - xm)^2$ = 0.01	0.0003	0.0009	0.0014	0.0012	0.0008	0.0000	0.0008	0.0026	0.0048

Sum (x − xm)(y − ym)	= −0.35	0.00	−0.01	−0.03	−0.03	−0.04	0.00	−0.01	−0.08	−0.14
Slope	= −27.45									
Intercept	= 25.19									
R	= 0.94									
R^2	= 0.88									
Residual	= 0.16	0.31	0.18	0.01	0.00	0.39	0.14	0.21	0.03	0.03
Standard error	= 0.40									
Comparative results										
Assessment revenue from bonus space		542	1,107	1,277	1,916	5,212	7,958	11,221	13,953	16,679
Assessment revenue difference from hypothetical change in average valuation		−4,339	−4,109	−2,205	−2,264	−161	−4,729	−7,060	−17,534	−21,064
Total net benefit		−3,796	−3,001	−927	−347	5,051	3,229	4,161	−3,581	−4,385
Net present value of benefit stream		−3,301								

Adapted from Kayden (1978).

to question, at least the order of magnitude of the impact has been identified. In reality, assessments are affected by a number of other economic and political factors, and the simplifying assumptions above may not conform to the true situation. The model provides a good approximation, however, and the strength of its results makes the further investigation of these theoretical difficulties even more interesting.

Multivariate analysis, or the use of several independent variables, is sometimes successful in pinning down estimates such as these with greater precision, but the analyst might not be able to deliver a definitive improvement in the level of predictive accuracy that really justifies the additional costs of using the techniques. Machine and software costs are minor, but multivariate models require more data, causing an attendant increase in the costs of data collection, cleaning, and transliteration. The additional skills and time needed to build and interpret multivariate models are also more costly, and the results of these more complicated constructions may be difficult to explain to people with little statistical background. In general, the more readily quantified the dependent variable and the greater the clarity of the causal relationships between independent and dependent terms, the better the likelihood that a multivariate model will be cost effective. A good example of this rule is the increasing use of multiple regression methods for estimating property values for local *ad valorem* taxation purposes. Market data on property sales is available from a number of private and public sources, and most of the determinants of property value, although far from definitively specified, can be isolated from one another and tested—again, using values from the field.

Multivariate models require more specialized statistical software, such as SPSS, SAS, or SOLIR. Only a limited number of observations can be stored in a spreadsheet format, and editing entries of this type is tedious. Moreover, spreadsheet programming is not optimized to perform large regression runs, unlike specialized packages. This significantly increases the time needed to set up and execute the regression problem. On the other hand, dedicated statistical packages offer a wide range of capabilities of which regression is only one. Data entry is generally uncomplicated, and files used in other programs, such as spreadsheets, can often be imported to statistical packages without requiring another key entry.

Conclusion

Planners faced with projection and forecasting tasks also face an important tradeoff between accuracy and expense. The microcomputer has certainly reduced data processing costs, but personnel costs still limit the time that managers can allocate to collecting data, creating models, and interpreting results. For many problems, models based on gross methodological simplifications are inappropriate, but on the other hand, the time needed for improving ballpark estimates may be a luxury that local governments cannot afford. No single policy can be recommended here, especially because the microcomputer has so dramatically expanded our analytic frontiers. Again, the responsibility for situational judgment rests on the analyst.

This is not a new dilemma. Fifteen years ago, great expectations were held for sophisticated systems of multisectoral projection and forecasting models, linked together to simulate the evolution of urban housing, employment, and land use markets. The amount of manpower this required was enormous, not only for collecting data and calibrating equations but also for initially structuring relationships between these components of change, using theory of far less than satisfactory explanatory value. Such model-making is useful but primarily for improving our theoretical understanding of urban systems. In the meantime, the ubiquitous and unchanging limitations on the resources of local government and the urgency of glimpsing even partial impressions of our most likely futures will urge us toward simpler microcomputer-based models that can be used here and now.

References

Bernstein, Samuel J., ed. 1978. *Selected Readings in Quantitative Urban Analysis.* Oxford: Pergammon Press.

Catanese, Anthony J. 1972. *Scientific Methods for Urban Analysis.* Urbana, Ill.: University of Illinois Press.

Isard, Walter. 1975. *Introduction to Regional Science.* Englewood Cliffs, N.J.: Prentice-Hall.

Isserman, Andrew M. 1984. "Projection, Forecast and Plan. *Journal of the American Planning Association* 50:208–221.

Kayden, Jerold S. 1978. *Incentive Zoning in New York City: A Cost-Benefit Analysis.* Cambridge, Mass.: Lincoln Institute of Land Policy.

Sipe, Neil G., and Robert W. Hopkins. 1984. *Microcomputers and Economic Analysis: Spreadsheet Templates for Local Government.* Gainesville, Fl.: Bureau of Economic and Business Research, University of Florida.

Wonnacott, Thomas H., and Ronald J. Wonnacott. 1972. *Introductory Statistics for Business and Economics.* New York: John Wiley.

Yeates, Maurice H., and Barry J. Garner. 1971. *The North American City.* New York: Harper & Row.

5

Fiscal and Budgetary Analysis

Neil Sipe

This chapter provides a compilation of several fiscal and budgetary analysis techniques that can be employed in a local government setting. Because many managers perceive local government budgets to be the substance of local development plans, it is important to review cost-effective analysis methods. The techniques described here will aid managers both in measuring the effects of changes in budgetary goals and policy and in evaluating the effects of land use changes.

This chapter also describes how a microcomputer can be used to speed the execution of these techniques. While all of these techniques have been in existence for many years, they have not been widely used because of the time involved in collecting the data and performing the calculations. The fiscal impact analysis described here requires more than 400 calculations. To perform such an analysis by hand would take more time than most planners have. However, by using a microcomputer and a spreadsheet template, the user needs only to collect and input the data.

Software packages such as Visicalc, Lotus 1-2-3, and Multiplan provide the microcomputer equivalent of an accountant's blank spreadsheet form. The numbers and equations for making calculations must be entered into the spreadsheet to make it useful, but once these equations are in place, all the calculations are performed automatically, saving time and reducing errors. Ease of calculation makes the microcomputer spreadsheet especially convenient for analyzing alternatives, using so-called what-if analyses. The user can easily change one or more input variables and almost instantly see the results.

The equations and constants entered into a spreadsheet program form what is called a template. The equations, numbers, or labels are entered in an individual cell of the spreadsheet. A cell is one of the blocks formed by the row/column grid. Once created, templates can be saved on a diskette and reloaded into the spreadsheet package whenever needed. This chapter describes seven templates that perform a variety of fiscal analyses. All templates are illustrated with examples drawn from Florida, where they were developed. Any sense of parochialism thus conveyed (since like all states, Florida's government has some unique features) should be outweighed by the advantage of concrete demonstration of the models in action.

Governmental Budget Analysis

The budget analysis template examines trends in a local government's annual revenues and expenditures. Simple and compound growth rates are computed, with and without an adjustment for inflation. Not only is the template useful for determining growth rates, but it is a good tool for seeing how much variation exists among four commonly used methods for describing growth or decline.

Required data

To use this template, the analyst must enter revenue and expenditure data for the current year and a previous budget year in cells C13 through D25 of template 1. Accounting categories change from time to time; therefore, it is important to be sure that the categories being compared contain the same items. To adjust for inflation, the gross national product (GNP) deflator must be input in cells C27 through D27. GNP deflators for the past ten years are shown in Table 5.1. For other years not shown, the *Survey of Current Business* should be consulted.

Table 5.1
Implicit Price Deflators for Gross National Product

Year	*GNP*
1972	100
1973	106
1974	115
1975	126
1976	132
1977	140
1978	150
1979	163
1980	179
1981	195
1982	207
1983	215

Source: U.S. Department of Commerce, Bureau of Economic Analysis (1984).

	A	B	C	D	E	F	G	H
1								
2	BUDGET ANALYSIS TEMPLATE							
3	Version 10/25/84 Print							
4	Bureau of Economic & Business Research							
5								
6	ENTER THE FOLLOWING DATA:							
7								
8	BEGINNING YEAR------>		1976					
9	ENDING YEAR--------->		1982					
10								
11	REVENUES		1976	1982				
12	---------------------------		----------	----------				
13	PROPERTY TAX		7002465	18636537				
14	OTHER LOCAL TAX		218254	53789				
15	UTILITY		2706286	4886949				
16	INTERGOVERNMENTAL		8114908	7546363				
17	MISCELLANEOUS		10949479	5160927				
18								
19	EXPENDITURES							
20	---------------------------		----------	----------				
21	GENERAL GOVERNMENT		8943766	10648806				
22	PUBLIC SAFTEY		5613011	11295101				
23	TRANSPORTATION		3052537	4076169				
24	UTILITIES		1658104	744709				
25	MISCELLANEOUS		8450708	6275548				
26								
27	GNP DEFLATOR		132	207				
28								
29	==========	==========	==========	==========	==========	==========	==========	==========
30								
31							SIMPLE %	COMPOUND
32					SIMPLE	COMPOUND	CHANGE IN	% CHANGE
33					PERCENT	PERCENT	CONSTANT	IN CONSTANT
34	REVENUES		1976	1982	CHANGE	CHANGE	DOLLARS	DOLLARS
35	----------	----------	----------	----------	----------	----------	----------	----------
36	PROPERTY TAX		7002465	18636537	27.69%	17.72%	11.62%	9.22%
37	OTHER LOCAL TAX		218254	53789	-12.56%	-20.82%	-14.05%	-26.54%
38	UTILITY		2706286	4886949	13.43%	10.35%	2.53%	2.38%
39	INTERGOVERNMENTAL		8114908	7546363	-1.17%	-1.20%	-6.78%	-8.34%
40	MISCELLANEOUS		10949479	5160927	-8.81%	-11.78%	-11.66%	-18.16%
41								
42	TOTAL		28991392	36284565	4.19%	3.81%	-3.37%	-3.69%
43								
44								
45	EXPENDITURES							
46	----------	----------	----------	----------	----------	----------	----------	----------
47	GENERAL GOVERNMENT		8943766	10648806	3.18%	2.95%	-4.01%	-4.49%
48	PUBLIC SAFTEY		5613011	11295101	16.87%	12.36%	4.72%	4.24%
49	TRANSPORTATION		3052537	4076169	5.59%	4.94%	-2.47%	-2.64%
50	UTILITIES		1658104	744709	-9.18%	-12.49%	-11.89%	-18.81%
51	MISCELLANEOUS		8450708	6275548	-4.29%	-4.84%	-8.77%	-11.71%
52								
53	TOTAL		27718126	33040333	3.20%	2.97%	-4.00%	-4.47%

Template 1.

Methodology

The change in each revenue and expenditure category is calculated as a simple growth rate and a compound growth rate. Since inflation is included in this calculation, the real change in revenue and expenditure patterns is overstated. Through the use of the GNP deflator, the two budgets can be restated in constant dollars to show the real growth (or decline) in individual categories.

Using the property tax category in cells A36 through H36, the methodology for each of the growth rates is shown below:

Simple percentage of change = ((Present property tax/past property tax) − 1)/(ending year − beginning year)
= 27.69%

Compound percentage of change = ((Present property tax/past property tax)^ (1/(ending year − beginning year))) − 1
= 17.72%

Simple percentage of change (constant dollars) = (((Present property tax/present GNP deflator)/(past property tax/past GNP deflator)) − 1)/(ending year − beginning year)
= 11.62%

Compound percentage of change (constant dollars) = (((Present property tax/present GNP deflator)/(past property tax/past GNP deflator))^ (1/(ending year − beginning year))) − 1
= 9.22%

The most significant feature of this template is to demonstrate how rates of growth or decline can be presented. In this example, depending on the method used, growth in property tax revenues ranged from 9.22 to 27.69 percent.

The results from this analysis can be helpful in understanding the fiscal impact template described below. Because that template is driven by per capita revenues and expenditures, it is important to know which revenue and expenditure categories are growing and which are declining. The budgetary categories used in this template are illustrative only. The categories can be changed, expanded, or contracted to suit individual needs. The template can also be used to examine growth rates for other items, such as population, income, and employment.

Fiscal Impact Analysis

The fiscal impact analysis template allows the user to examine the effects of a land use change on local government and school district operating revenues and expenditures.

Required Data

To analyze a residential project, two sets of data are needed. One deals with the project, and the other with local government. The project data are divided into two sections: (1) the direct data (cells C13 through C21 of template 2) include beginning and ending year of the project, inflation rate, persons per household, children per household, and percentage of rental, vacation, or seasonal units; (2) the indirect data (cells C25 through C30) required to examine the indirect impacts include persons per household, children per household, average home value, percentage living in rental units, and indirect multiplier.

While most of these required inputs can be obtained from the development proposal, one requires some additional explanation. The indirect multiplier represents the relationship between population growth and employment. In other words, given an increase of 1,000 people, how many new jobs will be created? The multiplier in the example is .51. This means that an increase of 1,000 people would result in 510 new jobs. Because the employment multiplier varies from area to area, it should be calculated for each jurisdiction (most likely county) in which the template is used.

The last required project data items are the number and price of residential units. If the project contains a wide variety of prices, enter the weighted average sales price. These data are entered in cells C37 through D46.

The local government data consist of the following items:

Per capita revenues
- local taxes
- intergovernmental/revenue sharing
- utility/charges for services
- miscellaneous

Per capita expenditures
- general government
- public safety
- utility
- transportation
- miscellaneous

Annual per student expenditures

Other local government data
- general government millage
- school millage
- assessment ratio

	A	B	C	D	E	F	G	H	I	J	K	L
1												
2	FISCAL IMPACT ANALYSIS: RESIDENTIAL											
3	Version 10/25/84											
4	Bureau of Economic & Business Research											
5												
6												
7	AS CURRENTLY CALIBRATED: TOTAL PER CAPITA REVENUES --->					126.38						
8		TOTAL PER CAPITA EXPENDITURES--------------->				195.25						
9												
10												
11	ENTER THE FOLLOWING DATA:											
12	------------------------		---------									
13	BEGINNING YEAR ------>		1985									
14	COMPLETION YEAR ------>		1986									
15	INFLATION (.XX) ------>		0.00%									
16												
17	CHARACTERISTICS OF EMPLOYEES:											
18	------------------------		---------									
19	PERSONS/HOUSEHOLD--->		2.45									
20	CHILDREN/HOUSEHOLD -->		0.47									
21	% RENTAL UNITS		50.0%									
22												
23	INDIRECT/INDUCED DATA:											
24	------------------------		---------									
25	PERSONS/HOUSEHOLD--->		2.6									
26	CHILDREN/HOUSEHOLD -->		0.5									
27	AVERAGE HOME VALUE -->		50000									
28	% LIVING IN RENTAL											
29	UNITS -------------->		50.00%									
30	INDIRECT MULTIPLIER --->		0.51									
31												
32												
33												
34			NO. OF	SALES								
35			HOMES	PRICE								
36			------	------								
37	1985	-------->	100	60000								
38	1986	-------->	100	60000								
39	0	-------->										
40	0	-------->										
41	0	-------->										
42	0	-------->										
43	0	-------->										
44	0	-------->										
45	0	-------->										
46	0	-------->										
47												
48			1985	1986	1987	1988	1989	1990	1991	1992	1993	1994
49	DEMOGRAPHICS - DIRECT											
50	------------------------		----------	----------	----------	----------	----------	----------	----------	----------	----------	----------
51	TOTAL POPULATION		246	492	492	492	492	492	492	492	492	492
52	SCHOOL CHILDREN		47	94	94	94	94	94	94	94	94	94
53												
54												
55	GENERAL GOVERNMENT - DIRECT											
56	------------------------		----------	----------	----------	----------	----------	----------	----------	----------	----------	----------
57	TAX BASE (000)		3615	7231	7231	7231	7231	7231	7231	7231	7231	7231
58												
59	REVENUES											
60	PROPERTY TAX		17386	34773	34773	34773	34773	34773	34773	34773	34773	34773
61	OTHER TAXES		4268	8536	8536	8536	8536	8536	8536	8536	8535	8536
62	INTERGOVT		18332	36664	36664	36664	36664	36664	36664	36664	36664	36664
63	UTILITY		4268	8536	8536	8536	8536	8536	8536	8536	8536	8536
64	MISC		4221	8443	8443	8443	8443	8443	8443	8443	8443	8443
65			----------	----------	----------	----------	----------	----------	----------	----------	----------	----------
66	SUBTOTAL		48476	96952	96952	96952	96952	96952	96952	96952	96952	96952
67												
68	EXPENDITURES											
69	GENERAL GOVT		16701	33402	33402	33402	33402	33402	33402	33402	33402	33402
70	PUBLIC SAFTEY		7656	15311	15311	15311	15311	15311	15311	15311	15311	15311
71	UTILITY		6723	13446	13446	13446	13446	13446	13446	13446	13446	13446
72	TRANSPORTATION		2374	4748	4748	4748	4748	4748	4748	4748	4748	4748
73	MISC		14578	29156	29156	29156	29156	29156	29156	29156	29156	29156
74			----------	----------	----------	----------	----------	----------	----------	----------	----------	----------
75	SUBTOTAL		48032	96063	96063	96063	96063	96063	96063	96063	96063	96063
76												
77												
78	NET BALANCE		444	889	889	889	889	889	889	889	889	889
79												
80												
81	SCHOOL BOARD - DIRECT											
82	------------------------		----------	----------	----------	----------	----------	----------	----------	----------	----------	----------
83	REVENUES											
84	LOCAL		24926	49853	49853	49853	49853	49853	49853	49853	49853	49853
85	STATE		67708	135416	135416	135416	135416	135416	135416	135416	135416	135416
86			----------	----------	----------	----------	----------	----------	----------	----------	----------	----------
87	SUBTOTAL		92635	185269	185269	185269	185269	185269	185269	185269	185269	185269
88												
89	EXPENDITURES		96726	193452	193452	193452	193452	193452	193452	193452	193452	193452
90												
91	NET BALANCE		-4091	-8183	-8183	-8183	-8183	-8183	-8183	-8183	-8183	-8183
92												

Template 2.

	A B	C	D	E	F	G	H	I	J	K	L
93											
94	DEMOGRAPHICS - INDIRECT										
95											
96	NEW JOBS	0	125.5	250.9	250.9	250.9	250.9	250.9	250.9	250.9	250.9
97	TOTAL POPULATION	0	326.2	652.4	652.4	652.4	652.4	652.4	652.4	652.4	652.4
98	SCHOOL CHILDREN	0	25.5	51.0	51.0	51.0	51.0	51.0	51.0	51.0	51.0
99											
100											
101	GENERAL GOVERNMENT - INDIRECT										
102											
103	TAX BASE (000)	0	3519	7037	7037	7037	7037	7037	7037	7037	7037
104											
105	REVENUES										
106	PROPERTY TAX	0	16921	33841	33841	33841	33841	33841	33841	33841	33841
107	OTHER TAXES	0	5660	11319	11319	11319	11319	11319	11319	11319	11319
108	INTERGOVT	0	24308	48616	48616	48616	48616	48616	48616	48616	48616
109	UTILITY	0	5660	11319	11319	11319	11319	11319	11319	11319	11319
110	MISC	0	5598	11195	11195	11195	11195	11195	11195	11195	11195
111											
112	SUBTOTAL	0	58145	116290	116290	116290	116290	116290	116290	116290	116290
113											
114	EXPENDITURES										
115	GENERAL GOVT	0	22145	44291	44291	44291	44291	44291	44291	44291	44291
116	PUBLIC SAFTEY	0	10151	20302	20302	20302	20302	20302	20302	20302	20302
117	UTILITY	0	8915	17830	17830	17830	17830	17830	17830	17830	17830
118	TRANSPORTATION	0	3148	6296	6296	6296	6296	6296	6296	6296	6296
119	MISC	0	19330	38661	38661	38661	38661	38661	38661	38661	38661
120											
121	SUBTOTAL	0	63690	127380	127380	127380	127380	127380	127380	127380	127380
122											
123											
124	NET BALANCE	0	-5545	-11089	-11089	-11089	-11089	-11089	-11089	-11089	-11089
125											
126											
127	SCHOOL BOARD-INDIRECT										
128											
129	REVENUES										
130	LOCAL	0	24258	48517	48517	48517	48517	48517	48517	48517	48517
131	STATE	0	36735	73471	73471	73471	73471	73471	73471	73471	73471
132											
133	SUBTOTAL	0	60994	121988	121988	121988	121988	121988	121988	121988	121988
134											
135	EXPENDITURES	0	52479	104958	104958	104958	104958	104958	104958	104958	104958
136											
137	NET BALANCE	0	8515	17030	17030	17030	17030	17030	17030	17030	17030
138											
139											
140	TOTALS (DIRECT+INDIRECT)										
141											
142	POPULATION	246.0	818.2	1144.4	1144.4	1144.4	1144.4	1144.4	1144.4	1144.4	1144.4
143	GOVERNMENTAL BALANCE	444	-4656	-10200	-10200	-10200	-10200	-10200	-10200	-10200	-10200
144	SCHOOL BOARD BALANCE	-4091	332	8847	8847	8847	8847	8847	8847	8847	8847
145											
146											
147											
148	LOCAL GOVERNMENT DATA:										
149											
150	PER CAPITA REVENUES										
151	LOCAL TAXES	-------->	17.35								
152	INTERGOVT AID	-------->	74.52								
153	UTILITY	-------->	17.35								
154	MISC	-------->	17.16								
155											
156	PER CAPITA EXPENDITURES										
157	GENERAL GOVT	-------->	67.89								
158	PUBLIC SAFTEY	-------->	31.12								
159	UTILITY	-------->	27.33								
160	TRANSPORTATION	-------->	9.65								
161	MISC	-------->	59.26								
162											
163	PER STUDENT EXPENDITURES										
164	ANNUAL COSTS	-------->	2058								
165											
166	OTHER LOCAL GOVERNMENT DATA										
167	GENERAL GOVT MILLAGE	-------->	4.809								
168	SCHOOL MILLAGE	-------->	6.8945								
169	ASSESSMENT RATIO	-------->	90.1								
170											
171	OTHER MODEL CONSTANTS										
172	STATE CONTRIBUTION TO										
173	SCHOOLS	-------->	0.7								
174	HOMESTEAD EXEMPT	-------->	25000								
175	COST-OF-SALE FACTOR	-------->	0.1								
176											
177											
178											
179											
180											
181											
182											
183											
184											

Template 2 (continued).

Other model constants
  state contribution to schools
  homestead exemption
  cost of sale factor

These data are entered at the end of the template in cells D151 through D175.

The user should exercise caution in calculating the local government data. There should be a reasonable balance between the per capita revenues and expenditures. Because the revenues do not include property tax receipts, they should be less than the expenditures. In the example, the total per capita revenues are $126.38, and the expenditures are $195.25. If there is not a reasonable balance between these two, any analysis undertaken will be biased. If total per capita revenues are far greater than expenditures, most projects will be fiscally positive, while if per capita expenditures are significantly greater than revenues, most projects will result in fiscal deficits.

Once a reasonable balance between revenues and expenditures has been achieved, the user should make any necessary adjustments to reflect provision of services by the developer. For example, one may wish to reduce the governmental per capita expenditure for parks and recreation (included in the miscellaneous category, cell D161) by some percentage if the development includes recreational amenities that would tend to offset the costs of a government unit providing the same services. This can also be done with the other expenditure categories as well.

Because this template is designed to examine only the effects on the operating budget, the local government data should not include capital expenditures or revenues from bond sales. If it is not possible to exclude capital, the user should average revenues and expenditures over a period of years to lessen the impact of a large capital expenditure.

In some states the budget may be divided into several different fund types, such as general government or enterprise. If this is the case, it will be necessary to combine the fund types to calibrate the model. (In Florida the *Local Government Financial Report* has two fund types: governmental and enterprise. The governmental fund includes most governmental services, while the enterprise fund includes services operated for profit, such as electric, water, sewer, gas, and refuse services.)

The source of these data will vary from state to state. In Florida local government revenues and expenditures can be found in the *Local Government Financial Report,* which contains the audited financial statements from each unit of government in the state. In a state that does not have such a report, these data can be taken from the local government budget.

The annual student expenditure (D164), like the other expenditure items, should not include any capital expenditures. In Florida these data can be found in the Department of Education annual report, which contains detailed financial characteristics of all school districts. If such a report is not available, the local school district office should be able to provide an estimate.

The data under the "other local government data" heading relate to property taxation. All data items in the category can be obtained from the property appraiser. The general government millage should be the millage that applies to the area in which the project is located. Thus if a project is located in a special taxing district, the millage appropriate for that district should be used. The school district millage, like the general government millage, should be millage that applies where the project is located.

The assessment ratio is the ratio of market value to assessed value. In Florida and many other states, property taxes are assessed at full market value. Thus the assessment ratio should be 100 percent; however, the actual ratio varies from county to county. In some states, property tax may not be assessed at full market value. In these instances the appropriate percentage should be used.

There are three items in the other model constants category. The first of these is the state contribution to schools. This factor is used in place of an education funding formula. In many states this formula is quite complex and requires a considerable amount of data. This template uses a percentage figure as an estimate of the state contribution to the local school district. In the example, the state provides .7 (or 70 percent) of the educational cost of each student. This percentage can be obtained from the local school board or can be calculated from the school budget.

Another model constant is the homestead exemption. In Florida all owner-occupied housing units receive an exemption of $25,000 on property taxes. For states without homestead exemptions a 0 would be used, while states with an exemption would enter the appropriate amount.

The last model constant is the cost-of-sale factor. In Florida the property appraiser deducts the costs of sale (real estate commission) from the assessed valuation. This factor varies from county to county, with 10 percent being the average. For states where the cost of sale is not a factor in property appraisal, a 0 should be used.

Methodology

The calculations are divided into three sections: (1) the direct analysis examines the direct impacts of the residential project on the local government budget; (2) the indirect analysis looks at the indirect or induced impacts of the project; and (3) the totals section combines the results of the direct and indirect analyses.

Direct Analysis. This section is divided into demographics, general government, and school board. The demographics section shows the total and school-age population. They are calculated as illustrated below:

Total population = (Units built) * (persons per household)
= 246

School-age population = (Units built) * (children per household)
= 47

The general government section is comprised of four areas: tax base, revenue, expenditures, and net balance. The tax base (cells A57 through L57) is a calculation of the total assessed valuation less the exemptions and cost of sale. This should not be confused with property tax revenues. The assessed valuation is the value on which the millage is applied to obtain property tax revenues. It is calculated as shown below:

Assessed valuation = ((Units built) * (unit price) (1 – cost of sale) * (assessment ratio/100)) – ((units built) * (1 – percentage rental) * (homestead exemption))
= $3,615,400

The revenues section (cells A59 through L66) is divided into five categories: property tax, other local tax, intergovernment, utility, and miscellaneous. While this is basically a per capita approach to fiscal impact analysis, the property tax revenues are based on actual project data, not per capita property tax revenues. The property tax is calculated as follows:

Property tax = (Assessed valuation) * (general government millage/1,000)
= $17,386

The millage is input as dollars of tax per $1,000 of assessed valuation. In the example, the property tax millage of 4.809 yields $4.809 per $1,000 of assessed valuation. Thus for a home assessed at $100,000, the property tax would be $480.90.

The other four revenue categories are calculated using the per capita methodology. The calculations for each are shown below:

Other taxes = (Per capita other local taxes) * (population)
= \$4,268

Intergovernment = (Per capita intergovernmental revenue) * (population)
= \$18,332

Utility = (Per capita utility revenue) * (population)
= \$4,268

Miscellaneous = (Per capita miscellaneous revenue) * (population)
= \$4,221

The total revenues in the first year of the project would be equal to the sum of the five categories. In this example the result would be \$48,476.

The expenditures section (cells A68 through L75) is divided into five categories: general government, public safety, utility, transportation, and miscellaneous. Each of these is calculated using the per capita methodology as shown below:

General government = (Per capita general government expenditure) * (population)
= \$16,701

Public safety = (Per capita public safety expenditure) * (population)
= \$7,656

Utility = (Per capita utility expenditure) * (population)
= \$6,723

Transportation = (Per capita transport expenditure) * (population)
= \$2,374

Miscellaneous = (Per capita miscellaneous expenditure) * (population)
= \$14,578

The total expenditures for the first year would be equal to the sum of these five categories, or \$48,032.

The net general government balance is the difference between the revenues and expenditures and is calculated as follows:

Net balance = (Revenues) − (expenditures)
= $444

General government impacts for subsequent years are calculated using the same methodology described above, substituting the population for the appropriate year. Thus in the second year the population from cell D51 would be used in the equations in place of cell C51.

The school board section is divided into three areas: revenues, expenditures, and net balance. The revenues section (cells A83 through L87) is divided into two categories: local and state. The local school board revenues are calculated as shown:

Local revenues = (Assessed valuation) * (school millage per 1,000)
= $24,926

The other revenue component is state funding. As noted above, state educational funding formulas tend to be quite complex. In this model a "state contribution to schools" factor is used in lieu of the educational funding formula. This factor is the percentage of student expenditures that the state provides. State revenues are calculated as follows:

State revenues = (Number of students) * (student expense) * (state contribution factor)
= $67,708

Thus the total school board revenues for the first year would be $92,635.

The school district expenditures are simply calculated as shown below:

Expenditures = (Number of students) * (annual student cost)
= $96,726

The net school district fiscal balance would be the difference between revenues and expenditures:

School board balance = (Revenues) − (expenditures)
= −$4,091

To calculate school board impacts for subsequent years, the same methodology as described above would be used, substituting the appropriate number of students for each year. Thus in the above example, cell D52 would be substituted for cell C52.

Indirect Analysis. As noted previously, the indirect analysis examines the impact of increased employment resulting from the addition of new housing units in a community. The format of the indirect portion of the template is similar to that of the direct analysis. There are a few differences, however. First, in the demographics section, an additional item has been entered: new jobs (cells A96 through L96). This represents the increase in employment due to new residential construction. It is calculated as follows:

$$\text{New jobs} = (\text{Project population}) * (\text{indirect multiplier}) = 125.5$$

Another difference is the lag. Because the indirect impacts depend on the direct residential construction, there is a one-year lag between the time a housing unit is occupied and the time when indirect impacts occur.

The methodology for the indirect calculations is similar to that described for the direct analysis, the only difference being the population that drives the analysis. For the indirect analysis, the total population in cells A97 through L97 is used rather than that in cells A51 through L51. Likewise the school population in cells A98 through L98 is used in place of that in cells A52 through L52.

Totals. This section of the template, shown in cells A142 through L144, merely combines the results of the direct and indirect analyses. The calculations for each component are described below:

$$\text{Population} = (\text{Direct}) + (\text{indirect}) = 246$$

$$\text{Governmental balance} = (\text{Direct}) + (\text{indirect}) = \$444$$

$$\text{School balance} = (\text{Direct}) + (\text{indirect}) = -\$4{,}091$$

A number of changes can be made to customize the template for individual situations. First, the present template is limited to projects with build-out periods (the length of development) of ten years or less. In some large-scale projects the build-out period may be twenty or thirty years. To increase the length of analysis, two things must be changed: the number of homes and sales price input section (cells C37 through D46) must be increased, and the results section (cells C48 through L144) should be increased to reflect the additional years. To do this, carefully replicate the formulas in cells L48 through L144.

Another change involves adding or deleting revenue and expenditure categories. In some situations it may only be necessary to have one revenue and one expenditure category. To do this the user would have to change the local government input section (cells D151 through D175) to reflect the altered categories as well as change the results section (cells C60 through L73 and cells C106 through L119).

While the model was originally designed for use in Florida, it can be changed for use in other states with little effort. The main difference is in tax-base calculation (cells C57 through L57 and C103 through L103). To apply this analysis in other states, the method of property tax calculation will have to be changed.

Estimating Capital Costs of Water Treatment

The following template allows the user to estimate the capital costs of constructing water treatment facilities. It can be used as an aid in determining future water treatment costs for a capital improvements plan, or it can be used to determine the effect of a single project.

Required Data

The data required for this analysis can be divided into four areas: water use, project description, financing, and cost update. In the water use area (cells D10 through D11 of template 3), three pieces of information are needed: residential water use per capita, nonresidential water use per employee, and excess treatment capacity. Residential water use generally ranges between 100 and 125 gallons per capita. Nonresidential water use, on the other hand, tends to be quite variable. The excess treatment capacity data item is the amount, if any, of excess capacity in the existing water treatment facility.

Three data inputs are needed in the project description area (cells D16 through D18). These include total number of new housing units, average household size, and total number of new employees. If the template is used to examine only a residential project, the new employee data should be 0. On the other hand, if the project has no residential component, the total number of new housing units would be entered as 0.

Large capital expenditures are seldom made in one lump sum; instead most governmental units sell bonds and annualize the debt over many years. The financing assumptions (cells D22 through D24) are used in determining the annual costs. These data include the annual interest rate, the length of the bond, and bond finance charges. The interest rate is dependent on several factors, including market conditions and the local government bond rating. The average interest rate for AAA-

	A	B	C	D	E	F	G
1							
2	CAPITAL COSTS OF WATER TREATMENT TEMPLATE						
3	Version 10/25/84 Print						
4	Bureau of Economic & Business Research						
5							
6	INPUT THE FOLLOWING INFORMATION						
7							
8	WATER DATA						
9	--						
10	RESIDENTIAL WATER USE PER CAPITA ----->			125			
11	NONRESIDENTIAL WATER USE/EMPLOYEE--->			200			
12	EXCESS TREATMENT CAPACITY (mgd) ----->			0.02			
13							
14	PROJECT DESCRIPTION						
15	--						
16	TOTAL NUMBER OF NEW HOUSING UNITS --->			1700			
17	AVERAGE HOUSEHOLD SIZE --------------->			2.4			
18	TOTAL NUMBER OF EMPLOYEES ----------->			50			
19							
20	FINANCING ASSUMPTIONS						
21	--						
22	INTEREST RATE (.XX) ------------------>			12.00%			
23	LENGTH OF BOND (YEARS) --------------->			20			
24	BOND FINANCE CHARGES (.XX) ----------->			15.00%			
25							
26	COST UPDATE FACTOR						
27	--						
28	CURRENT GNP DEFLATOR ---------------->			207			
29							
30							
31							
32							
33							
34							
35							
36		PACKAGE-COMPLETE PLANT		INTERMEDIATE-SIZED FACILITIES		LARGE TREATMENT PLANT	
37		(FLOWS LESS THAN .5 MGD)		(FLOWS BETWEEN .5-1.0 MGD)		(FLOWS > 1.0 MGD)	
38	WATER FLOW	----------------------------		----------------------------		----------------------------	
39	(MGD)	TOTAL ($)	ANNUAL ($)	TOTAL ($)	ANNUAL ($)	TOTAL ($)	ANNUAL ($)
40	----------	----------	----------	----------	----------	----------	----------
41	0.50	*N/A	*N/A	617288	95038	*N/A	*N/A
42							
43							
44							
45							
46							
47							
48							
49							
50							
51							
52							
53							

Template 3.

rated municipal bonds can be found in the St. Louis Federal Reserve Bulletin. For municipal bonds with lower ratings the general rule of thumb is a twenty-five to fifty basis-points (.25 to .50 percent) increase for each level below AAA. Thus if the AAA-rated bond interest rate is 11.50 percent, the interest rate for an A-rated bond (two levels below AAA-rated bonds) would range from 12.00 to 12.50 percent. The local government bond rating can be found in *Moody's Municipal Bond Ratings* or *Standard and Poor's Ratings.*

The last financing data item is bond finance charges. When bond financing is contemplated, there are a number of additional items that must be included: capitalization of the first year's interest, which can amount to 15 percent of the total bond issue; financial underwriter charges (10 percent of the issue); and charges for printing and bond counsel (5 percent of the issue). It is essential to include these items in the bond issue.

The cost update factor (cell D28) is used to adjust the cost functions for the appropriate year. In the example, the cost function is adjusted for 1982. To update these functions for future years it is necessary to input the appropriate GNP deflator. The GNP deflator is discussed under "Government Budget Analysis" above.

Methodology

Users of this technique should be aware of its limitations. Estimated costs are assumed to be for the construction of new facilities and not for additions or expansions to existing treatment facilities. It is not possible to develop a generalized model that would take into account the feasibility of increasing the capacity of existing treatment facilities. Another, corollary assumption is that a new facility is constructed for each project. Because of these limitations, the template is not suited to estimate the actual water treatment impacts of a specific project. It is, however, a good tool for comparing development projects on their relative impacts. The best use for this template is in the determination of long-term water treatment costs, such as those made for a capital improvement plan.

The methodology for determining capital costs of water treatment systems was taken from Deb (1982b). In that study, treatment costs for more than sixty unit processes were determined. These processes were grouped in three categories: those appropriate for flows of 0 to .5 million gallons per day (mgd); those for flows of .5 to 1.0 mgd; and those for flows above 1.0 mgd. Before estimates of water treatment costs can be made, the expected water flow must be calculated. The methodology is described below:

Water flow = ((((Residential water use) * (number of homes * household size)) + ((nonresidential water use) * (number of employees)))/1,000,000) − existing capacity
= .50g

The equations for the treatment processes can be written so that the appropriate treatment process is used based on the calculated water flow. To do this, the user should include a conditional statement (not shown below) so that if the flow is not appropriate for a process, an "NA" will appear, as shown in the example in cells A41 through C41 and F41 through G41.

For a 0 to .5 mgd facility, the following cost function representing a package-complete treatment plant is used:

Cost = (((433,000) * (water flow ^ .43)) + 60,000) * (cost update factor/207)
= (((433,000) * (A41 ^ .43)) + 60,000) * (D28/207)

In the example the water flow is greater than .5 mgd; therefore, this treatment process is not appropriate. The methodology for determining the annual cost is described below:

Annualized cost = (Total cost * (1 + bond finance charge)) * (interest rate/(1 – ((1 + interest rate) ^ (– length of bond))))
= (B41 * (1 + D24)) * (D22/(1 – ((1 + D22) ^ (– D23))))

The intermediate-size facility utilizes a combination of three unit processes: rapid mix and coagulation, clarification, and gravity filtration. Combining the cost functions for these unit processes yields the following:

Cost = (((63,300) * (water flow ^ .45)) + (((180,000) * (water flow ^ .51)) + 8,600) + ((670,000) * (water flow ^ .62))) * (cost update factor/207)
= 616,309

The difference between the figure calculated above and that in template 3, cell D41, is due to rounding error.

The annualized cost formula is identical to that shown above except that the total cost would be taken from cell D41 rather than B41.

For those facilities treating more than 1.0 mgd, the following processes were combined: flash mix and coagulation, sedimentation, filtration, chlorination equipment, and chlorine contact tank. A combination of these cost functions results in the following equation:

$$\begin{aligned}\text{Cost} &= (((209{,}640) * (\text{water flow} \,\hat{}\, .685)) + ((162{,}255) * (\text{water flow} \,\hat{}\, .893)) + ((667{,}400) * (\text{water flow} \,\hat{}\, .63)) + ((11{,}056) * (\text{water flow} \,\hat{}\, .822) + 8{,}328) + ((40{,}492) * (\text{water flow} \,\hat{}\, .725) + 4{,}308)) * (\text{cost update factor}/207) \\ &= (((209{,}640) * (\text{A41} \,\hat{}\, .685)) + ((162{,}255) * (\text{A41} \,\hat{}\, .893)) + ((667{,}400) * (\text{A41} \,\hat{}\, .63)) + ((11{,}056) * (\text{A41} \,\hat{}\, .822) + 8{,}328) + ((40{,}492) * (\text{A41} \,\hat{}\, .725) + 4{,}308)) * (\text{D28}/207)\end{aligned}$$

Since the water flow in template 3 is less than 1 mgd, this formula would not be appropriate for estimating treatment costs.

The annualized cost formula is identical to that shown above, again substituting the appropriate total cost from cell F41.

The cost functions used here represent only a few of the many different combinations of treatment processes. While the template utilizes the three processes described above, additional processes and the associated cost curves can be included to represent any standard treatment process. Descriptions of other treatment processes can be found in Deb (1982b).

Estimating Capital Costs of Wastewater Treatment

The next template permits the user to make estimates of the capital cost of wastewater treatment facilities. Similar to the water treatment template, it can be used to determine future wastewater treatment costs for a capital improvement program or to determine the impact of a single residential or nonresidential project.

Required Data

There are four categories of required data: wastewater generation rates, population/location, financing assumptions, and cost updates. In the first section (cells D9 through D11 of template 4) three data items are needed: residential and nonresidential wastewater generation per capita and excess treatment capacity. Wastewater generation can be determined by examining water use. If residential water use is 125 gallons

	A	B	C	D	E	F	G	H	I
1	CAPITAL COSTS OF WASTEWATER TREATMENT TEMPLATE								
2	Version 10/25/84 Print								
3	Bureau of Economic & Business Research								
4									
5	INPUT THE FOLLOWING INFORMATION								
6									
7	WASTEWATER DATA								
8									
9	RESIDENTIAL GENERATION (gal./capita) ------------>			100					
10	NONRES. GENERATION (gal./employee) ------------>			160					
11	EXCESS TREATMENT CAPACITY ------------------>			0.03					
12									
13	PROJECT/LOCATION DATA								
14									
15	TOTAL NUMBER OF NEW HOUSING UNITS------------->			2500					
16	AVERAGE HOUSEHOLD SIZE ---------------------->			2.4					
17	TOTAL NUMBER OF EMPLOYEES ------------------>			200					
18	REGIONAL ADJUSTMENT FACTOR ----------------->			0.75					
19									
20	FINANCING ASSUMPTIONS								
21									
22	INTEREST RATE (.XX) ------------------------>			12.00%					
23	LENGTH OF BOND (YEARS) ---------------------->			20					
24	BOND FINANCE CHARGES (.XX) ------------------->			15.00%					
25									
26	COST UPDATE FACTOR								
27									
28	CURRENT GNP DEFLATOR ----------------------->			215					
29									
30									
31				SECONDARY TREATMENT				ADVANCED TREATMENT	
32				WITH NUTRIENT REMOVAL		ADVANCED		WITH NUTRIENT REMOVAL	
33		SECONDARY TREATMENT		(FOR FLOWS > .29)		WASTE TREATMENT		(FOR FLOWS > .49)	
34	WASTEWATER FLOW								
35	(MGD)	TOTAL ($)	ANNUALIZED ($)	TOTAL ($)	ANNUALIZED ($)	TOTAL ($)	ANNUALIZED ($)	TOTAL ($)	ANNUALIZED ($)
36									
37	0.60	1984265	305499	2027752	312194	2333442	359258	2408752	370853

Template 4.

per capita per day, then the wastewater generation rate should be approximately 100 gallons per capita per day. In other words, wastewater generation is about 80 percent of the water use. However, this will tend to vary from region to region and state to state. This same factor can be used to determine the nonresidential rate as well.

The population/location category (cells D15 through D18) consists of four data items: total number of new households, average household size, total number of new employees, and the regional adjustment factor. Most of these items are self-explanatory; however, one requires some explanation. The adjustment factor takes into account regional variations in construction costs. All costs are normalized, with Kansas City, Missouri, being 1.00. In north and central Florida, for example, where costs are less than in Kansas City, there is an adjustment factor of .75. Thus calculated treatment-plant costs are reduced by 25 percent.

The third and fourth sections are identical to those found in the water treatment template discussed above.

Methodology

The methodology for determining wastewater treatment costs is taken from the U.S. Environmental Protection Agency (1980). The cost curves used here were developed from a data base that includes more than 730 treatment plants in the United States. These costs represent the entire project cost, including construction, administration, legal, architecture and engineering, contingencies, and planning. All cost curves are calibrated in 1978 dollars. The cost update factor allows the user to update these costs for the current year.

The user should be aware of the limitations of this template. It is assumed that the estimated costs are for the construction of new facilities and not for additions or expansions to existing facilities. Because of this limitation the template tends to overestimate treatment plant costs for an individual project. The best use for this template is in the determination of long-term wastewater treatment costs—similar to what is needed for a capital improvement plan.

The first step involved in determining wastewater treatment is the calculation of the expected wastewater flow:

Flow (mgd) = ((((Residential flow per capita) *
(housing units * household size)) +
(nonresidential flow per employee *
number employees))/1,000,000) −
excess treatment capacity
= .60

Four levels of treatment are available in this module: secondary, advanced secondary with nutrient removal, advanced wastewater treatment (AWT), and AWT with nutrient removal. Two of the processes have some restrictions. The advanced secondary with nutrient removal can be used when flows are greater than .29 mgd, and the AWT with nutrient removal can be used when flows are greater than .49 mgd. The cost functions for each are shown below:

Secondary = ((2.66 * 1,000,000) * (wastewater flow ^ .72)) * (cost update factor/150) * regional adjustment
= $1,978,314

Secondary (nutrient removal) = ((2.76 * 1,000,000) * (wastewater flow ^ .75)) * (cost update/150) * regional adjustment
= $2,023,023

AWT = ((3.16 * 1,000,000) * (wastewater flow ^ .74)) * (cost update/150) * regional adjustment
= $2,326,404

AWT (nutrient removal) = ((3.52 * 1,000,000) * (wastewater flow ^ .89)) * (cost update/150) * regional adjustment
= $2,402,281

The difference between the figures calculated here and those in template 4, cells A37 through I37, is attributable to rounding error.

The template can be customized for individual jurisdictions by determining what treatment process is used and then inputting the appropriate cost curve in the template. For large jurisdictions with several treatment districts, the template could be expanded so that calculations could be made for each district.

Estimating Capital Costs of Water Distribution

The following template can aid users in calculating the costs of distributing water from the treatment facility to the consumer.

Required Data

The required data fall into four categories: existing conditions, future projections, financing assumptions, and cost update. In the existing-condition section (C10 through C12 of template 5) two data items are required: the population and the level-of-development multiplier. The population should be the existing population served by the present water distribution network. However, if it is not known, the current population of the jurisdiction can be substituted. The level-of-develop-

	A	B	C	D	E	F
1						
2	CAPITAL COSTS OF WATER DISTRIBUTION TEMPLATE					
3	Version 10/25/84 Print					
4	Bureau of Economic & Business Research					
5						
6	INPUT THE FOLLOWING INFORMATION:					
7						
8	EXISTING CONDITIONS					
9	------------------------------------		----------------------			
10	POPULATION ----------------->		162000			
11	LEVEL-OF-DEVELOPMENT					
12	MULTIPLIER --------------->		1.5			
13						
14	FUTURE PROJECTIONS					
15	------------------------------------		----------------------			
16	EXPECTED POPULATION -------->		2000			
17	HOUSEHOLD SIZE -------------->		2.4			
18	UNITS/ACRE------------------>		4.0			
19						
20	FINANCING ASSUMPTIONS					
21	------------------------------------		----------------------			
22	INTEREST RATE (XX)----------->		12.00%			
23	LENGTH OF BOND--------------->		20			
24	BOND FINANCE					
25	CHARGES (XX) ------------->		15.00%			
26						
27	COST UPDATE FACTOR					
28	------------------------------------		----------------------			
29	CURRENT GNP DEFLATOR -------->		215			
30						
31						
32	LENGTH OF		AVERAGE			
33	ADDITIONAL		DIAMETER OF		TOTAL CAPITAL COSTS	
34	WATER LINES		WATER LINES		TOTAL	ANNUALIZED
35	(MILES)		(INCHES)		DOLLARS	DOLLARS
36	--------------		------------		----------	----------
37	4.62		13.53		1104452	170042
38						
39						
40						
41						
42						
43						
44						
45						
46						
47						
48						
49						
50						
51						
52						
53						

Template 5.

ment multiplier relates to the character of the area being developed. The costs of laying pipe are much higher in developed areas than in rural or undeveloped areas. Deb (1982b) has found that the cost of installing pipe in urban or suburban areas is twice that of installation in an undeveloped area. Thus if the area under consideration is urban or suburban, the user would enter a 2 for this multiplier to double the installation costs. For an undeveloped area a 1 would be used, and costs would not be affected. If the character of the area falls somewhere between developed and undeveloped, a factor between 1 and 2 can be used—for example, 1.4.

The second category (C16 through C18) deals with future projections. Three data items are needed: expected population, household size, and units per acre.

The third section (C22 through C25), financing assumptions, requires three data items: annual interest rate, length of the bond, and bond finance charges. For more discussion of these factors see the "required data" section in the discussion of "estimating capital costs of water treatment."

The last category is the cost-update factor entered in C33. Again the user is referred to the "required data" section of the water treatment template for more discussion.

Methodology

The methodology for this template is based on that described in Deb (1982b). The water distribution system consists of all pipes and appurtenances in the system from the treatment plant to the end user. Before proceeding, the user should be aware of the limitations of this approach: (1) Because this methodology takes into account the smaller distribution lines within subdivisions normally provided by the private sector, the costs will tend to be overestimated; (2) the methodology is geared to examine residential water supply, not industrial applications; (3) the template is intended to give a general idea of costs; it should not be substituted for detailed engineering estimates.

To estimate distribution system cost, one must know all the pipe diameters as well as their respective lengths. If, however, the lengths and diameters are unknown, a simplified procedure as described here can be used. To determine the length of water line required, Deb (1982b) found that a relationship exists between population density and total length of the water lines. As the population density increases, the amount of water line needed per person decreases. Through analysis of water systems throughout the nation the following relationship was derived:

$$\begin{aligned}\text{Length in miles} &= 125.39 * (\text{population density per square mile} \wedge .458) * \text{population in thousands}\\ &= 4.62 \text{ (for the illustrated case)}\end{aligned}$$

The user should note that the population density and the population are for the project and not for existing conditions.

The diameters of the pipes are determined in a different manner. The diameter is defined as an average of all the various pipe sizes in the total distribution network. This average increases with the population of the service area. By examining a host of water systems throughout the country the following relationship was derived:

$$\begin{aligned}\text{Average diameter (inches)} &= 6.2 * (\text{total population}) \wedge .065\\ &= 13.53\end{aligned}$$

Once the length and average diameter have been determined, the capital cost can be estimated using the following relationship:

$$\begin{aligned}\text{Cost} &= (1.01 * (\text{diameter} \wedge 1.29) * (\text{length} * 5{,}280)) * (\text{level-of-development multiplier}) * (\text{cost-update factor}/207)\\ &= \$1{,}105{,}425\end{aligned}$$

The difference between the figure calculated above and that in template 5, cell E37, is due to rounding error.

The annualized cost is calculated as follows:

$$\begin{aligned}\text{Annualized cost} &= (\text{Total cost} * (1 + (\text{bond finance charge})) * (\text{interest rate}/(1 - ((1 + \text{interest rate}) \wedge (-\text{bond length})))))\\ &= \$170{,}346\end{aligned}$$

This template could be set up to examine various districts within a water service area. To do this the user would have to change the input section so that data (level of development, population, household size, and units per acre) for each district could be entered.

Estimating Capital Costs of Wastewater Collection

The next template (template 6) estimates the capital costs of wastewater collection lines.

Required Data

There are four categories of required data: wastewater, project/location, financing assumptions, and cost update. The wastewater data section (cells D9 through D15) consists of six data items: residential wastewater flow per capita, nonresidential flow per employee, interceptor sewer length, distance between pump stations, pump station cost, and excess capacity in lines already in place. The estimates of wastewater flow per capita and per employee should be based on estimated water use. The interceptor sewer length can be determined in a number of ways—by measuring the distance on a map or by actually surveying the distance—but these methods are not always feasible. The methodology used here requires an estimate of the length in feet per capita. The EPA suggests the following: collector sewers—16 feet per capita; interceptor sewers—1 foot per capita.

Collector sewers are found within subdivisions and are usually provided by the private sector. The interceptor sewers are much larger in diameter and are generally provided by the public sector. These per capita factors are valid only in a best-case situation. When a new project is located miles from the nearest interceptor, the actual distance should be input and not the per capita estimate.

Depending on the terrain of the area, pump stations may be required. Generally the number of pump stations cannot be estimated until considerable engineering has been done. The EPA (U.S. EPA 1980) recommends one pump station of 1.2 mgd capacity for each 65,000 feet of interceptor sewer. The cost of such a pump station is estimated to be $248,068 in 1982 dollars. If the user has better estimates for either the number of pump stations required or their cost, they should be input in place of the EPA estimates.

The project per location category (cells D19 through D23) is made up of five data items: total number of new housing units, average household size, level-of-development multiplier, number of new employees, and regional adjustment factor. The level-of-development multiplier is similar to that used for the water treatment templates; however, the size of the multiplier is smaller. The EPA (U.S. EPA 1980) estimates that this multiplier should be 1.15 for urban situations, .90 for suburban areas, and .75 for rural areas.

The regional adjustment factor is the same as that used in the wastewater treatment template. The third and fourth sections (cells D27 through D29 and D33) of data are the same as those found in the other capital-cost templates discussed above.

	A	B	C	D	E
1	CAPITAL COST OF WASTEWATER COLLECTION TEMPLATE				
2	Version 10/25/84 Print				
3	Bureau of Economic & Business Research				
4					
5	INPUT THE FOLLOWING INFORMATION				
6					
7	WASTEWATER DATA				
8	--			------------	
9	WASTEWATER FLOW PER CAPITA ---------------->			100	
10	NONRESIDENTIAL FLOW/EMPLOYEE -------------->			160	
11	INTERCEPTOR SEWER LENGTH				
12	IN FEET/CAPITA --------------------------->			1	
13	DISTANCE BETWEEN PUMP STATIONS (ft) ---------->			64000	
14	PUMP STATION COSTS -------------------------->			248068	
15	EXCESS SYSTEM CAPACITY (MGD) ---------------->			0.01	
16					
17	POPULATION/LOCATION DATA				
18	--			------------	
19	TOTAL NUMBER OF NEW HOUSING UNITS ------------>			1700	
20	AVERAGE HOUSEHOLD SIZE ------------------------>			2.4	
21	LEVEL OF DEVELOPMENT MULTIPLIER -------------->			1.15	
22	NUMBER OF NEW EMPLOYEES --------------------->			50	
23	REGIONAL ADJUSTMENT FACTOR ------------------>			0.75	
24					
25	FINANCIAL ASSUMPTIONS				
26	--			------------	
27	INTEREST RATE (.XX)---------------------------->			12.00%	
28	LENGTH OF BOND (YEARS)------------------------>			20	
29	BOND FINANCE CHARGES (.XX)-------------------->			15.00%	
30					
31	COST UPDATE FACTOR				
32	--			------------	
33	CURRENT GNP DEFLATOR ------------------------>			207	
34					
35					
36		REQUIRED		CAPITAL COSTS	
37	ADDITIONAL	PIPE	AVERAGE	(1982 $'s)	
38	WASTEWATER	DIAMETER	INSTALLED	------------------------	
39	FLOW (MGD)	(INCHES)	COST/FOOT	TOTAL	ANNUALIZED
40	------------	------------	------------	------------	------------
41	0.41	12	58.65	258233	39758
42					
43					
44		LOOKUP TABLE		LOOKUP TABLE	
45		FOR DIAMETER		FOR COST	
46	0	8	0	40.54	
47	0.2	10	8.1	50.89	
48	0.3	12	10.1	58.65	
49	0.5	15	12.1	73.31	
50	0.7	18	15.1	94.88	
51	1.1	21	18.1	113.85	
52	1.5	24	21.1	128.51	
53	2.1	27	24.1	148.35	
54	2.8	30	27.1	159.56	
55	3.5	36	30.1	193.20	
56	5.5	42	36.1	260.48	
57	7.7	48	42.1	309.64	
58	10.1	54	48.1	361.39	
59	12.9	60	54.1	457.13	
60	17.2	66	60.1	479.55	
61	20.6	72	66.1	599.44	
62	26.4	72	72.1	599.44	
63					

Template 6.

Methodology

The methodology used to determine wastewater collection system costs is taken from EPA (U.S. EPA 1981). This methodology and the cost functions are based on detailed analyses of more than 700 wastewater systems throughout the United States. The user should be aware of the limitations of this methodology. The costs estimates are only as good as the input data. The estimates of wastewater flow and length of pipe are important in obtaining reasonable costs. The methodology for determining the wastewater flow is shown below:

Flow = (((Housing units * people per household * residential flow per capita) + (number of new employees * nonresidential flow per employee))/1,000,000) − excess capacity
= .41 mgd

Once the wastewater flow is calculated, then the required pipe diameter can be estimated. The lookup table in cells A46 through B62 is used in this determination. The numbers in cells A46 through A62 represent wastewater flows from 0 mgd to 26.4 mgd, while the numbers in cells B46 through B62 are the estimated pipe diameters for these flows. In the example the flow is .39 mgd, which falls between .3 (cell A48) and .5 (cell A49). The estimated pipe diameter is then taken from cell B48, which is the pipe size for flows of .3 to .5 mgd. Thus in this case the pipe diameter is 12 inches, which is shown in cell B41.

The average installed cost (cell C41), inclusive of all appurtenance, nonpipe construction, and engineering and design costs, is also determined with a lookup table. The numbers in cells C46 through C62 represent pipe diameters, while the costs for the installation of each of these diameters are shown in cells D46 through D62. (Apple users may place the lookup table in cells A66 through B82 to aid in calculation.) In the example, the estimated diameter is 12 inches, which corresponds to an installed cost as shown below:

Installed cost = Normalized cost in 1982 dollars * (present GNP deflator/207) * level-of-development multiplier * regional adjustment factor
= $58.65 per foot

This lookup table is different from the one in cells A46 through B62 in that the costs (cells D46 through D62) can be updated and adjusted based on the year, the level of development, and the regional location.

The total capital costs are determined as illustrated below:

Total cost = (((Number of residential units * household size) + number of employees) * average installed cost per foot * length of sewer line per capita) + (((((number of residential units * household size) + number of employees) * length of sewer line per capita)/distance between pump stations) * pump station cost)
= $258,233

The annual costs based on the total are calculated as shown below:

Annual cost = (Total cost * (1 + bond finance charges)) * (interest rate/(1 − ((1 + interest rate) ^ (− length of bond))))
= $39,758

Since the unit costs for the collection system depend on a number of factors including diameter, burial depth, and type of pipe, average costs are used here. If the user has better cost or engineering standards applicable to the local area, they should be used.

Estimating Capital Costs for Police, Fire, Libraries, and Parks and Recreation

The final template is intended to aid users in assessing the effects of new residential development on local government capital expenditures for police, fire, parks and recreation, and libraries.

Required Data

This template requires two categories of data: project/location data and expenditure data. The project/location section (cells D10 through D12 of template 7) consists of the current population of the jurisdiction, the total number of new housing units, and the average household size.

The expenditure-data category (cells D16 through D19) requires total (capital + operating) expenditures for police, fire, parks and recreation, and library. These data can be obtained from the local government budget or the individual department heads.

	A	B	C	D	E	F	G	H
1								
2	CAPITAL COSTS FOR OTHER PUBLIC FACILITIES TEMPLATE							
3	Version 10/25/84 Print							
4	Bureau of Economic & Business Research							
5								
6	ENTER THE FOLLOWING DATA.							
7								
8	POPULATION/LOCATION DATA							
9	----------	----------	----------	----------				
10	CURRENT POPULATION -------------->			250000				
11	TOTAL # OF NEW HOUSING UNITS ---->			2000				
12	AVERAGE HOUSEHOLD SIZE ----------->			2.3				
13								
14	EXPENDITURE DATA							
15	----------	----------	----------	----------				
16	ANNUAL EXPENDITURE FOR POLICE---->			5000000				
17	ANNUAL EXPENDITURE FOR FIRE ------>			3000000				
18	ANNUAL EXPEND. FOR PARKS/REC. --->			50000				
19	ANNUAL EXPENDITURE FOR LIBRARIES->			100000				
20								
21								
22	NOTE:							
23	ASSUMES A TOTAL POPULATION OF:			254600				
24								
25								
26								
27	POLICE		FIRE		PARKS & REC.		LIBRARIES	
28	----------	----------	----------	----------	----------	----------	----------	----------
29	CAPITAL-	ANNUAL	CAPITAL-	ANNUAL	CAPITAL-	ANNUAL	CAPITAL-	ANNUAL
30	TO-OPER.	CAPITAL	TO-OPER.	CAPITAL	TO-OPER.	CAPITAL	TO-OPER.	CAPITAL
31	RATIO	EXPEND.	RATIO	EXPEND.	RATIO	EXPEND.	RATIO	EXPEND.
32	----------	----------	----------	----------	----------	----------	----------	----------
33	0.052	260000	0.047	141000	0.345	17250	0.034	3400
34								
35	ATTRIB. TO							
36	NEW GROWTH->	4698		2548		312		61
37								
38								
39								
40	LOOKUP TABLE		LOOKUP TABLE		LOOKUP TABLE		LOOKUP TABLE	
41	FOR POLICE		FOR FIRE		FOR PARKS		FOR LIBRARIES	
42	----------	----------	----------	----------	----------	----------	----------	----------
43	0	0	0	0.099	0	0.269	0	0.001
44	2500	0.058	2500	0.018	2500	0	2500	0
45	5000	0.056	5000	0.05	5000	0.031	5000	0
46	10000	0.054	10000	0.026	10000	0.097	10000	0
47	25000	0.051	25000	0.022	25000	0.124	25000	0
48	50000	0.047	50000	0.029	50000	0.148	50000	0.031
49	100000	0.058	100000	0.063	100000	0.245	100000	0
50	200000	0.052	200000	0.047	200000	0.345	200000	0.034
51	300000	0.064	300000	0.043	300000	0.471	300000	0.04
52	500000	0.037	500000	0.049	500000	0.317	500000	0.044
53	1000000	0.062	1000000	0.407	1000000	0.32	1000000	0.407

Template 7.

Methodology

The methodology used for this template is based on Burchell and Listokin (1978). This methodology utilizes the ratio of operating-to-capital expenditures to determine future capital costs. While it is far better to estimate capital needs directly, this is a difficult task. As Table 5.2 shows, capital expenditures for these governmental services are small compared to those for other public services. These ratios are taken from Burchell and Listokin (1978) for cities in the 200,000 to 300,000 population range located in the southern United States. These authors have also developed ratios for all population ranges and geographic regions of the country, based on data collected from the Census of Local Governments in 1976.

What the figures in this table show is that sewerage, water supply, and highways tend to be capital-intensive services. For highways, with a ratio of 1.09, capital and operating costs are almost equal. For sewerage, with a ratio of 1.581, capital costs are more than one and a half times greater than operating costs. Police and fire services, on the other hand, tend to be labor intensive, with capital expenditures amounting to only 5.2 percent and 4.7 percent, respectively, of operating costs.

This methodology is limited in that local capital expenditures will, in the long term, be similar to existing expenditure patterns for cities and counties of similar size and location. Furthermore, the template is not appropriate for determining nonresidential impacts.

The capital costs for fire, police, parks and recreation, and libraries are estimated using two factors: the current annual expenditures and the capital-to-operating ratio. Burchell and Listokin (1978) have calculated these ratios for eleven different government sizes for different regions of the country. These ratios are input in the table in the form of lookup tables. The example has the capital-to-operating ratios for the southern United States.[1]

In the example, the jurisdiction has a population of 254,600 (cell D23). The capital-to-operating ratio for police is .052 (cell B50 of the lookup table). The annual capital expenditure would be calculated as shown below:

Police capital expenditure = Capital-to-operating ratio * total annual expenditure
= $260,000

[1]For users outside the South (Alabama, Arkansas, Delaware, Florida, Georgia, Kentucky, Louisiana, Maryland, Mississippi, North Carolina, Oklahoma, South Carolina, Tennessee, Texas, Virginia, Washington, D.C., and West Virginia), the capital-to-operating ratios in the lookup tables must be changed. The ratios for other parts of the country can be found in Burchell and Listokin (1978). The accuracy of this methodology can be enhanced by the addition of county- or city-specific capital- to-operating ratios. These ratios can be calculated by examining the local government budget over a period of five to ten years and determining the ratio of capital expenditures to operating expenditures.

Table 5.2
Capital-to-Operating Ratios for Various Governmental Functions

Sewerage	1.581
Water supply	1.206
Highways	1.090
Police	0.052
Fire	0.047

Thus the total capital expenditure for the police department is estimated to be $260,000. The calculation below shows the capital expenditures that would be attributable solely to the new growth.

Police capital expenditure (new growth) = (Total capital expenditure) * (number of new housing units * household size)/(total population) = $4,698

Summary and Cautions

The seven templates described above illustrate the usefulness of spreadsheet templates for fiscal and budgetary analysis. Templates, however, are not without their critics. Some say that templates are easy to abuse—that users can produce results without knowing what the results mean or how they were obtained. While this may be true, the same criticism can be made of hand calculators. To ensure that templates are used properly, it is critical that adequate documentation and explanation be provided. A second criticism of templates—particularly the models described here which calculate capital costs of water and wastewater systems—is that they are too general. Potential users should be cautioned that these templates are not to be used in place of detailed engineering studies. They are primarily intended for making ballpark estimates. More detailed templates can be produced, using these as models, to take into account additional data elements.

As the uses of microcomputers expand, so does the use of spreadsheets and spreadsheet models or templates. Unfortunately, some unanticipated problems have accompanied this expansion. Many of these problems are traceable to the template developer's failure to leave an adequate record of his or her objectives or procedures. Templates are a form of computer software, and without proper documentation they can be useless. It is important, therefore, to set standards for template development and documentation. Some organizations have evolved standard formats that all spreadsheet templates must follow. For example, specific areas of the template are defined for data input, documentation, and macros.

In addition to the on-screen documentation, it is advisable to set standards for printed documentation as well. The examples in this chapter illustrate an abbreviated documentation style. Several principles apply. First, the documentation should include a brief statement of purpose; in other words, it should say what the template is supposed to do. Second, if any data are required as input they should be described. The user should also be given an idea where these data can be obtained. Third, the methodology should be presented in detail. As this chapter illustrates, each critical formula must be described. Fourth, while not necessary, it is useful to describe steps that can be taken to update or customize the template. For example, the fiscal impact analysis described in this chapter is based on conditions in Florida; however, with some minor changes it can be modified for use in other states. Fifth, it is useful to provide references or background material, if available, to aid in understanding the template. In the case of the wastewater treatment template, much of the data and cost curves were obtained from Environmental Protection Agency studies.

Given these cautions and suggestions, the development and use of templates should become more efficient. At the same time, careful users should be able to avoid adverse consequences of overzealous application.

References

Burchell, Robert W., and David Listokin. 1978. *The Fiscal Impact Handbook: Estimating Local Costs and Revenues of Land Development.* New Brunswick, N.J.: The Center for Urban Policy Research.

Deb, Arun. 1978. *Multiple Water Supply Approach for Urban Water Management.* Washington, D.C.: National Science Foundation Grant ENV-18499.

———. 1982a. *Alternative Technologies for Small Water System Management* Washington, D.C.: National Science Foundation Grant 1SP 80 15075.

———. 1982b. *User's Manual for the Water Management (WATMAN) Model.* Washington, D.C.: National Science Foundation Grant 1SP 80 15075.

Division of Public Schools. 1983. *Profiles of Florida School Districts 1981–1982.* Tallahassee: Annual Report of the Commissioner of Education.

Fishkind, Henry H., Neil G. Sipe, and Jerome W. Milliman. 1983. *The Fiscal Impact Model.* Gainesville: Bureau of Economic and Business Research, University of Florida.

Florida Department of Banking and Finance. 1983. *State of Florida Local Government Financial Report, Fiscal Year 1981–82, Supplement: Revenue and Expenditure Detail.* Tallahassee: Department of Banking and Finance.

Milliman, Jerome W., Neil G. Sipe, and Robert W. Hopkins. 1983. *The Capital Needs Assessment Model.* Gainesville: Bureau of Economic and Business Research, University of Florida.

U.S. Department of Commerce, Bureau of Economic Analysis. 1984. *Survey of Current Business* 64(8).

U.S. Environmental Protection Agency. 1980. *Construction Costs for Municipal Wastewater Treatment Plants: 1973–1978.* Denver, Colo.: General Services Administration.

———. 1981. *Construction Costs for Municipal Wastewater Conveyance Systems: 1973–1979.* Denver, Colo.: General Services Administration.

6

Cost-Effective Geoprocessing Strategies

Alven H. S. Lam

Many planners still assume that maintaining a computerized geographic information system (GIS) in smaller local government offices is an expensive and complicated proposition. But recently developed technologies in microcomputer hardware and software have made it possible for even the smallest office to enjoy the benefits of an affordable, user-friendly, and efficient GIS. The multipurpose GIS is gradually being accepted as a primary base for urban or regional information systems used to assist planners in their day-to-day land-related or location-oriented decision making. Even inexperienced users can operate a microcomputer-based GIS to retrieve, analyze, and maintain spatial and nonspatial information.

One of the primary functions of local government is to establish appropriate mechanisms for monitoring area development. The goal, from an economic standpoint, is to maximize the benefits from the utilization of resources and to allocate these resources in the most appropriate way. Local policies regarding resource allocation are guided in part by national and regional policies in three major environments: political, socioeconomic, and physical systems. The first two of these are notoriously unstable, but their conditions are also easiest to read at local levels, as was shown in chapter 3. Indeed, socioeconomic conditions, changeable as they are, form the foundation on which political goals are built. To understand how these conditions interact with conditions in the physical environment and thereby affect the needs of particular regions, it is useful to analyze socioeconomic, environmental, and locational data concurrently. The key to formulating successful policies lies in combining and balancing concerns in each of these realms.

The streamlining of operational and managerial functions to support policy in each of these environments has been facilitated by the introduction of the microcomputer. New technology has upgraded possible applications from the level of word processing to information management and even to the more sophisticated level of policy analysis and decision making. Computers provide logical and analytical tools to assist people in analyzing information and making decisions more quickly, objectively, and comprehensively.

Geoprocessing is a decision support tool. It permits analysis and presentation of information in an aggregated and easily understandable form—a visual image, often a map. The visual output triggers further cycles of the interactive rethinking and reconsideration process that molds decisions. Two-dimensional and three-dimensional images are easier to understand than linear data in rows and columns.

Broadly defined, a GIS is a computerized data base management system that handles both attribute information and geographic information. Table 6.1 outlines the types of information and examples of relevant analytical tools used to better formulate policies and decisions on a wide variety of planning and development issues.

The left column of Table 6.1 lists examples of attribute information, such as population and average household income. These data describe the social and economic conditions of neighborhoods or other areas. Shift/share analysis, curve fitting, and multivariate analysis are examples of tools used to analyze existing conditions and to forecast future trends. Typical applications of attribute data manipulation are budget planning, economic growth management, and land use monitoring.

In the right column, geographic information is used to define the

Table 6.1
Attribute and Geographic Information Processing

	Attribute Information	*Geographic Information*
Data	Population Income Rent Land value Zoning	Point Line Polygon Network
Tools	Statistics Shift/share analysis Multivariate analysis Curve fitting Entropy maximizing	Cartographic modeling Spatial analysis Geometric modeling
Applications	Budget planning Economic growth analysis Migration analysis	Location analysis Environmental assessment Spatial distribution Physical impact analysis Land use monitoring

shape, size, and boundary of a physical environment. Basic elements on which geographic information are built include points, lines, and areas (polygons) or networks. In combination, these elements can describe any man-made or natural physical characteristic such as rivers, ground cover, property boundaries, rights-of-way, or voting wards. The linkage of geographic information and attribute information is important because land use planning and other growth management programs must be based on an analysis of both socioeconomic data and physical characteristics. The following applications use both geographic and attribute information.

Cartographic data modeling is a process for interpreting lines and surfaces based on sampling data. For instance, we can model a three-dimensional trend surface of estimated land value by using land value samples.

Spatial analysis is used to search out and summarize relationships between physical entities. For example, an environmental impact study may need an enumeration of the households located within a flood plain.

Geometric modeling generates abstract geometric shapes to outline a special area. For example, a 3,000-foot radius circle may be inscribed on a map to represent the impact area of a new pollution center.

A geoprocessing system may include any or all of the capabilities mentioned above, depending on the specific applications. Table 6.2 presents some examples of system costs and capabilities. A planning agency can consider itself a candidate for a microcomputer-based GIS if the following conditions are evident:

1. Location or land-related decisions are made on a daily basis.
2. Specially trained data processing personnel are not available.
3. Complicated geoprocessing is only occasionally required.
4. The jurisdiction uses only medium- or smaller-size data bases.
5. Management intends to efficiently train potential land information managers and analysts.
6. Information processing budgets are limited.

Based on the essential functions of local government agencies, three categories of geoprocessing applications—for land use planners, assessors, and utility managers—will be discussed, and evaluation criteria will be presented. This discussion will be followed by a case study of geoprocessing as a decision support tool.

Table 6.2
Microcomputer Geoprocessing Software and Hardware

	Atlas	*Geo-Graphics*	*Multimap*	*SOLIR*	*Microtrip*
Computer	IBM PC/XT	TEKTRONIX 4050	IBM PC/XT	IBM PC/XT	IBM PC/XT
Graphic resolution	Medium	High	Medium	Medium	Medium
Plotter	Yes	Yes	Yes	Yes	Yes
Digitizer	No	Yes	Yes	Yes	No
Memory	192K	64K	256K	256K	128K
Interface	1-2-3	—	DBMS	SOLIR	UTPS, DBMS
Cartographic modeling					
Thematic mapping	Yes	Yes	Yes	Yes	No
Vector-grid conversion	No	No	No	No	No
Contour map	No	No	No	No	No
Trend surface	No	No	No	No	No
Spatial analysis					
Point-in-polygon	No	No	No	Yes	No
Overlay	No	No	No	No	No
Spatial search	No	No	No	Yes	No
Network	No	No	No	Yes	Yes
Geometric modeling					
Distance	No	No	No	No	Yes
Location	No	No	No	No	No
Intersection	No	No	No	No	No
Software cost	$339–449	$27,000+	$1,000–2,000	$750	$3,000

Geoprocessing for Land Use Planners

Land use planners must deal with many different kinds of geographic information, such as topological, soil, slope, zoning, and land use information. Inside this complicated world, planners not only have to keep physical characteristics in mind but also must understand the interrelationships among physical elements on similar, larger, or smaller scales. The major issues here are how to store, retrieve, and summarize different kinds of geographic information efficiently, as well as how to analyze the information to support decision making. Mapping and surface processing are two important geoprocessing techniques used by planners.

Mapping

Planners use maps to analyze neighborhood characteristics and to express their ideas and recommendations. Computerized mapping, which transforms source maps into a digital format, is therefore the most useful geoprocessing function. Two kinds of digital maps best respond to planners' needs.

Vector maps (such as topological maps, street maps, administrative boundary maps, planning area maps, zoning maps, railroad, water, and land use maps) are stored and displayed in vector form because precise boundary descriptions are most often required in planning operations. A vector map means the map data are stored as lines represented by strings of vectors, line segments, or X and Y coordinates. Figure 6.1 presents an example of a vector map that was produced by SOLIR, the Lincoln Institute of Land Policy's land management and geoprocessing software. The geoprocessing system also overlays attribute information, or socioeconomic figures, on top of geographic boundaries and creates thematic maps (see Figure 6.2). Other geographic information, such as rivers, railroads, or hazardous zones, can also be overlaid so that the physical relationships can be compared. Planners with this capability are better equipped to analyze area development potentials and the distributional consequences of decisions with spatial dimensions.

Grid maps are used when area boundary precision is not essential, as in regional planning or environmental impact studies. A grid map stores the map information in rectangular grid cells that have coordinates that are easily referenced. Each grid cell has its geographic references and corresponding attribute information. The advantages of a grid map are efficiency of processing, ease of vertical overlays, and other spatial search applications. A vector map can be displayed in a grid format by a

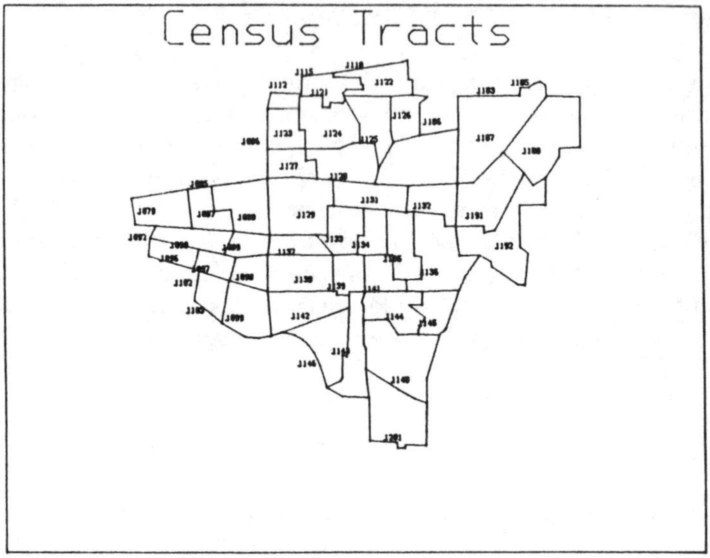

Figure 6.1. *Geographic data representation in vector format.*

two-step process that converts area boundaries first and then the value represented within the boundaries.

Methods used to overlay or combine grid maps displaying different shapes or values hinge on set manipulation (see Figures 6.3a and 6.3b). The logic functions used in set theory are Boolean operators AND, OR,

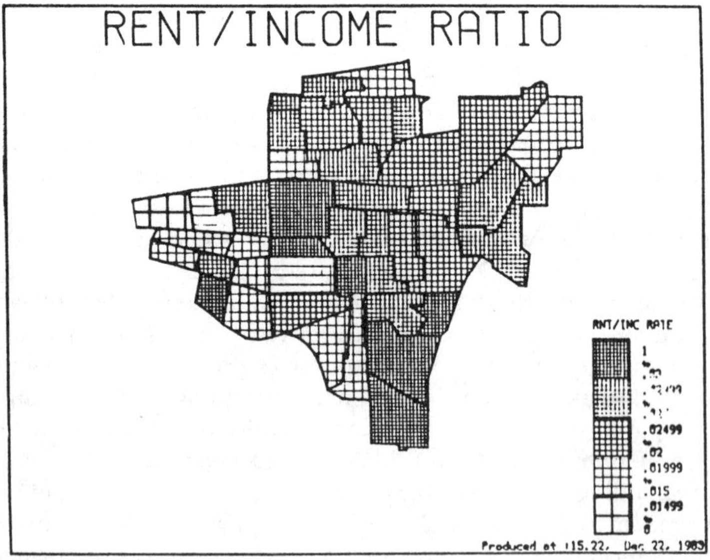

Figure 6.2. *Geographic and attribute data representation in vector format.*

a. b.

Figure 6.3. *Geographic data representation in grid format.*

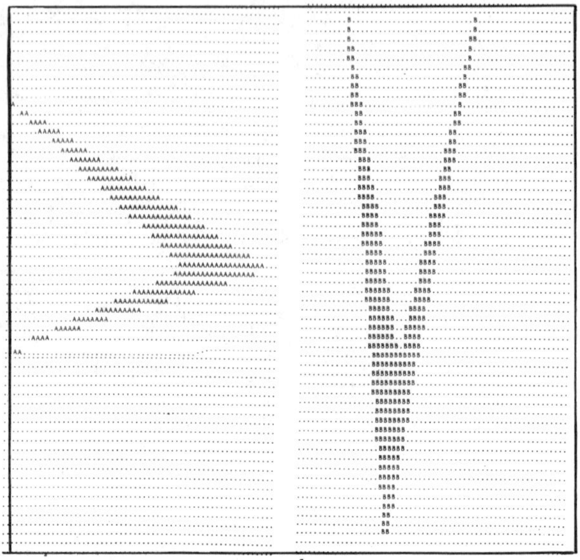

a. b.

Figure 6.4. *Set A in grid format (a); Set B in grid format (b).*

NOT, and XOR. If a polygon on a grid plane can be recognized as a "set," then using logic functions to manipulate one "set" in relation to others will result in polygon overlays. Sample sets A and B are shown in Figure 4a and Figure 4b respectively; Figures 4c, 4d, and 4e show the OR, AND, XOR functions applied to both grid maps. This technique creates quick polygon overlays that, for microcomputers, are needed to tackle more complicated geoprocessing problems.

Surface Processing

The other type of the geoprocessing capability of interest to the land planner is surface processing to analyze or present analog information in graphic form. Response surfaces are two- or three-dimensional representations generated from spatial information that let planners evaluate the general characteristics of an area. Trend surface and contour maps are frequently used to perform spatial comparisons and analyses.

A *trend surface* is generated by using the altitude of known control points to interpolate other unknown points. A two-dimensional surface is usually presented in grid form (Figure 6.5a), and a three-dimensional surface is usually displayed in vector form (Figure 6.5b). This is a time-consuming process because of the need for adequate surface resolution, as well as the processing time required by weighting and scaling algorithms.

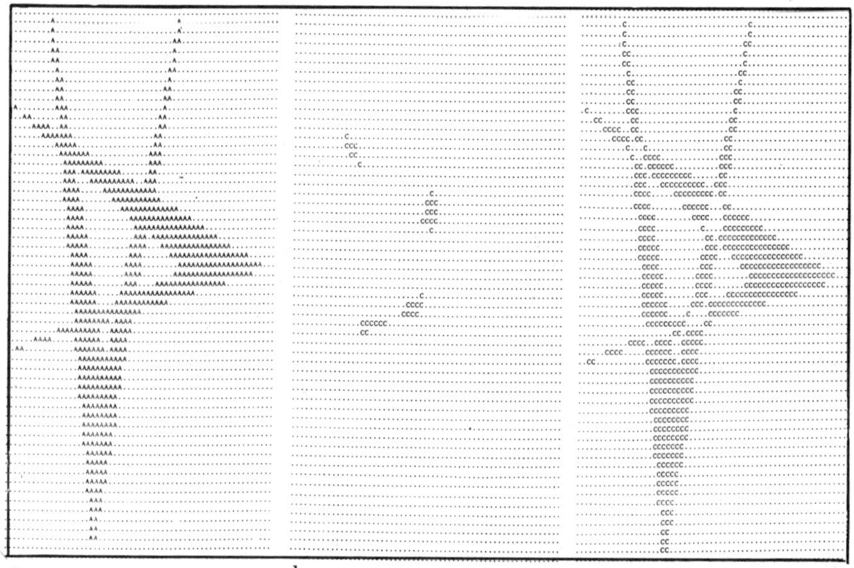

c. d. e.

Figure 6.4 (cont'd.). *"OR" function of set A and set B* (*c*); *"AND" function of set A and set B* (*d*); *"XOR" function of set A and set B* (*e*).

Contour maps are valuable for land planners because slope, orientation, and terrain roughness are key factors that affect development suitability. As in trend surfaces, contour maps can be presented in two-dimensional or three-dimensional forms. Two-dimensional maps need supplementary materials to indicate slope and other physical terrain data, but three-dimensional maps, although they provide better representations, have the disadvantages of slow processing and difficulty in integrating other spatial information (Figure 6.6).

Geoprocessing for Assessors

In the United States in 1979 there were 13,439 local government assessing units, and 77.7 percent of local tax revenue was generated from property taxes. The importance of property taxes and of modernization of assessment operations has been emphasized in local governments by the adoption of new technologies to improve the efficiency and effectiveness of assessment activities. Whereas land use planners work with a wide variety of map types and attribute data, local assessing authorities primarily need parcel-based information for taxation purposes.

Assessors' maps are traditionally used to show locations, dimensions, and configurations of individual parcels. The components of an assessor's map, usually used for legal descriptions, include parcel boundaries,

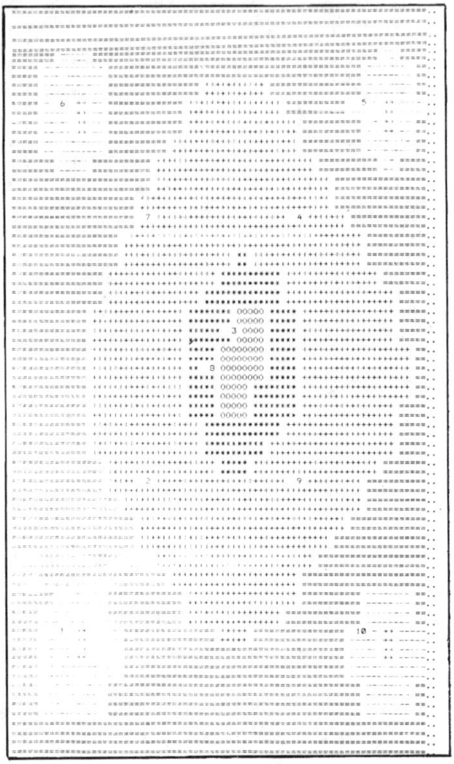

Figure 6.5a. *Two-dimensional surface processing in grid format.*

dimensions, bearings, subdivision names and boundaries, easement and right-of-way boundaries, location and name of street, parcel identifiers, and street address. Mapping these components requires accurate input and output devices in order to support legal statements. Recently assessors have been deriving wider functions from their maps, which have become "a data base that informs about the land, its geographic and non-geographic attributes, and about relationships among these attributes" (Costello and Garvin 1982). Maintaining an effective mapping system, or a multipurpose cadastral system, can assist assessors in monitoring their assessment activities by tracing transactions, collecting delinquencies, and performing mass appraisals and reappraisals of properties. Computer mapping can easily highlight interesting areas such as properties with tax delinquencies or properties with assessed values that are higher or lower than their selling prices.

There are two ways to store parcel maps: by digitizing aerial photos or source maps or by key entering "metes and bounds" from a land survey report. Either method has its advantages and disadvantages, depending on which has more accurate source information. The second

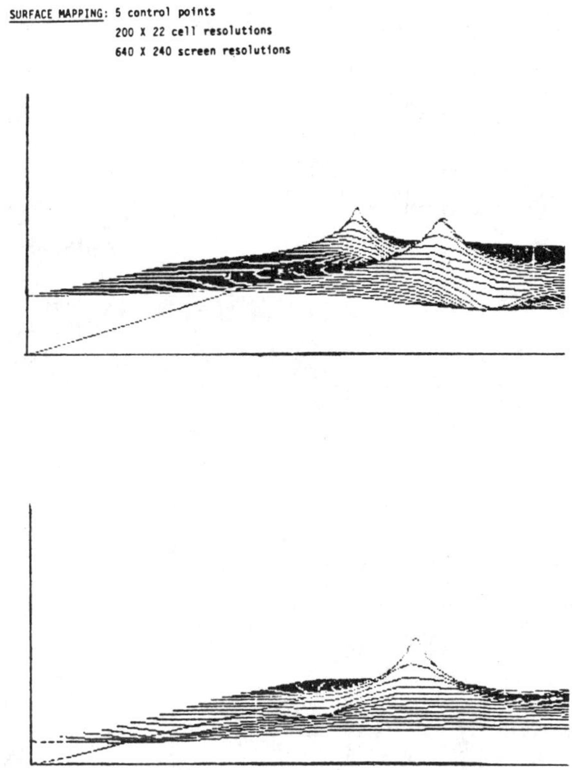

Figure 6.5b. *Three-dimensional surface processing in vector format.*

method generally results in less human error, and its data can be used for legal descriptions of property boundaries.

Accuracy requirements for parcel mapping are ±.35 feet, ±0.17 feet, and ±0.08 feet in rural areas, rural and urban ring areas, and urban areas, respectively (National Research Council 1982). Once the source maps are accurately surveyed and recorded at these standards, a computerized mapping system should be able to store and display these maps with the same accuracy standards. If a microcomputer cannot handle enough significant digits to process these numbers, or if an output device has less graphic resolution to meet the requirements, other written documentation or descriptions should be attached to the computer maps for legal purposes.

Currently developed microcomputer technology can assist local assessment offices in implementing their computerized property mapping programs. Smaller jurisdictions can now accommodate microcomputer-based data processing functions within limited budgets, and large jurisdictions can use microcomputers to decentralize critical functions so

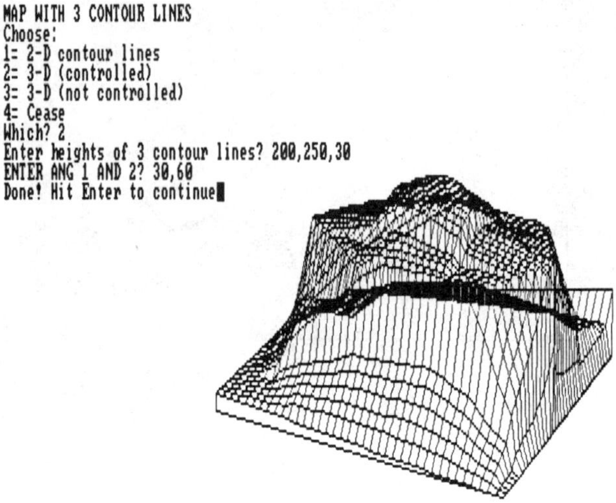

Figure 6.6. *Three-dimensional contour mapping.*

that large data bases can be maintained and shared by a wider user group.

Geoprocessing for Utility Managers

The availability of utility services is an important factor in evaluating land for development suitability or cost. Sophisticated utility management systems provide support to operational and managerial functions (design, maintenance and construction, and so forth) as well as more broadly based decisions regarding large resource allocations. Whenever an area or a particular location needs new facilities or infrastructure, utility managers must take into consideration the physical characteristics of the surrounding area, soil types, street rights-of-way, easement boundaries, and other utility systems.

Utility mapping assists managers in understanding the physical relationships of all different utility and infrastructure systems, whether underground or above the surface. The accuracy required, however, is higher than with other geoprocessing systems in terms of displaying, searching, or aggregating spatial data. Important information such as length, depth, width, and capacity is crucial when engineering design and maintenance are underway, so levels of specificity and resolution satisfactory to planners and assessors may not be sufficient for utility managers.

Evaluation of a Microcomputer Geoprocessing System

Each of the application environments described above has a unique mission that demands certain capabilities from a geoprocessing system. Still, all geoprocessing systems can be evaluated according to similar performance criteria; only the relative emphasis on individual factors will change. (Compare Tables 6.2 and 6.3.) Factors for evaluating and implementing a microcomputer geoprocessing system include:

1. *Hardware and software cost:* The hardware costs, including computer, storage device, printer, digitizer, and plotter, can total under $10,000. Software costs range from $600 to $3,000. Software falls into two categories: attribute data management ($300 to $800) and cartographic data base management ($300 to $2,000).
2. *System upgrading:* Microcomputer hardware and software is constantly evolving. Systems should be easily updated and upgraded without loss of data, delay of project schedules, or additional great expense for new hardware, software, and training.
3. *Data transfer capability:* Many geographic and cartographic data files are maintained on mainframe or minicomputers by the U.S. Bureau of the Census and the USGS. Importing those files, or parts of them, to a microcomputer mapping system greatly

Table 6.3
Mini- and Mainframe Computer Software

	Symap	*Calform*	*Odyssey*
Cartographic modeling			
Thematic mapping	Yes	Yes	Yes
Vector-grid conversion	Yes	No	No
Contour map	Yes	No	No
Trend surface	Yes	No	No
Spatial analysis			
Point-in-polygon	No	No	Yes
Overlay	No	No	Yes
Area search	No	No	Yes
Network	No	No	No
Geometric modeling			
Distance	No	No	No
Area	No	No	Yes
Intersection	No	No	Yes
Software cost	$1,500	$1,700	$10,000

simplifies the set-up process because fresh data gathering, editing, and error checking is expensive and time consuming.

4. *Compatibility with other systems:* Cartographic data and attribute data are usually maintained independently. There are many sophisticated attribute data base management systems, and a geoprocessing system can become more "knowledgeable" if it is interfaced with such a system. However, not all geoprocessing systems can access files from all attribute data base management systems.
5. *Geographic data accuracy:* Different geoprocessing applications require different levels of accuracy. A planner's map needs moderate levels of accuracy because the maps present spatial relationships or a comprehensive view of the spatial characteristics of geographic areas. An assessor's map is often used for legal functions and requires high accuracy capable of reflecting field survey results and other legal statements. Utility mapping, which affects engineering operation, construction, maintenance, and capital investment, needs the highest level of accuracy available in mapping systems.
6. *Data storage:* Storage space is critical when complex areas must be geoprocessed. Cartographic data, not to mention accompanying attribute files, are voluminous and may consume secondary storage space very quickly.
7. *Ease of learning and implementation:* Ease of learning techniques of map input, editing, labeling, scaling, windowing, and overlaying is an important factor in training nontechnical personnel. Ease of implementation is a variable that often dramatically affects project costs.

The horizon for microcomputer geoprocessing systems has rapidly expanded as new technologies are introduced. Computing speed, computer graphics algorithms, data retrieval algorithms, and graphic output devices are key elements of each system, and each is subject to improvement. It is important for users to keep up with these trends. Because the microcomputer is a practical tool for self-training and self-education, understanding the uses of computers and computer maps is the first and foremost consideration when choosing a system. If local officials are using computer mapping for planning, operation management, and policy stratification, they may find it worthwhile to implement a microcomputer-based geoprocessing system or a geographic information system in their daily operations.

Case Study: Geoprocessing Integrated into Decision Making

In October 1982 the Lincoln Institute of Land Policy and the city of Cleveland, Ohio, began a three-year collaborative effort to demonstrate how microcomputers can be used for storing and processing land-related information. One component of this effort was the collection of parcel and census tract data regarding the city's Enterprise Zone or, as it later became known, the Cleveland Target Redevelopment Area. The area is a mixed residential, commercial, industrial, and educational zone of approximately 13,000 parcels of land within forty-one census tracts. Simultaneously, the office of the mayor organized seven public- and private-sector advisory committees to prepare specific priorities for the target area. These committees addressed issues across a number of different sectors, including economic development, land use and development planning, community development, negotiated investment strategies, institutional frameworks, legislative review, and public information and marketing.

To illustrate the integration of decision-making strategies and geoprocessing tools, this chapter describes three methods that can be combined to facilitate conflict resolution and joint goal setting. These include a decision-making simulation technique, a site selection algorithm, and a thematic mapping routine. Each of these methods uses the microcomputer as a means of making the decision-making process more explicit. The illustrative materials are drawn from data bases established by the city of Cleveland. Even though the case here is hypothetical, the techniques can be applied in conjunction with complementary negotiation procedures in local government settings.

The Analytic Hierarchy Process

The first step in this example is to determine, through a simulation technique called the analytic hierarchy process (AHP), one set of redevelopment strategies favored most strongly by all of the appointed advisory committees. A total of eleven strategies were proposed by all of the groups (Figure 6.7), which were then asked to indicate their individual preferences for each strategy, in comparison to all others, on a scale of one to nine. Ratings are entered into a preference matrix for each group (Figure 6.8). An eigenvalue and an eigen vector are then computed on each preference matrix to linearize the priority of each actor. All priorities are compiled in a decision tree to ascertain overall preferences for each strategy (Figure 6.9). The three most preferred

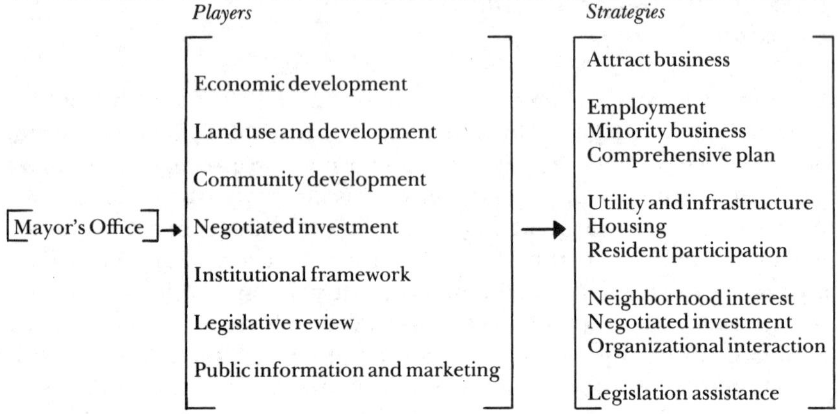

Figure 6.7. *Decision tree number 1—players and strategies.*

development strategies derived from this process include *assistance to minority business, upgrading utilities and infrastructure,* and *improving housing.*

The next step is to define consensus on the socioeconomic measures to be used in judging which subareas of the target area are in greatest need of development assistance, in the form of programs that respond to the selected strategies. Since census tracts are convenient subdivisions of the target area, eleven candidate census variables are proposed as criteria (Figure 6.10). A similar type of matrix is constructed by each committee (Figure 6.11) in order to rate their preferences for each criterion, and the results are summed to produce an aggregate rating for each measurement. The two most preferred measures are the unemployment rate and median gross rent (Figure 6.12).

Comparables Analysis

Choosing the subareas of greatest need is facilitated by a program called comparables analysis, which is part of the SOLIR software package. This routine identifies records in a data file (in this case, all target area census tracts) based on values of variables selected by the analyst. All of the eleven variables were used as selection criteria. The program also includes a feature that allows the analyst to weight the importance of each variable in the selection procedure, so results from the aggregate evaluation criteria preference matrix were entered into the algorithm.

Player 1: The Mayor

	A	B	C	D	E	F	G	PRIORITY
A. Economic Development	1.00	2.00	4.00	0.33	2.00	3.00	5.00	0.22
B. Land Use & Development	0.50	1.00	3.00	2.00	3.00	1.00	4.00	0.21
C. Community Development	0.25	0.33	1.00	0.33	0.50	0.50	2.00	0.06
D. Negotiated Investment	3.03	0.50	3.03	1.00	5.00	3.00	7.00	0.29
E. Institional Framework	0.50	0.33	2.00	0.20	1.00	1.00	2.00	0.08
F. Legislative Review	0.33	1.00	2.00	0.33	1.00	1.00	2.00	0.10
G. Public Info & Marketin	0.20	0.25	0.50	0.14	0.50	0.50	1.00	0.04

PRIORITY (HIGH TO LOW) = D A B F E C G

Player 2 : Economic Development

STRATEGIES

	A	B	C	D	E	F	G	H	I	J	K	PRIORITY
A. Attract Bus	1.00	1.00	3.00	4.00	3.00	5.00	7.00	4.00	1.00	2.00	3.00	0.11
B. Employment	1.00	1.00	2.00	3.00	4.00	5.00	5.00	4.00	2.00	4.00	5.00	0.14
C. Minority Bu	0.33	0.50	1.00	2.00	3.00	3.00	3.00	3.00	2.00	4.00	3.00	0.08
D. Comprehensi	0.25	0.33	0.50	1.00	2.00	1.00	2.00	2.00	4.00	3.00	5.00	0.10
E. Utility & I	0.33	0.25	0.33	0.50	1.00	1.00	0.50	0.33	0.25	2.00	0.33	0.05
F. Housing	0.20	0.20	0.33	1.00	1.00	1.00	3.00	2.00	2.00	3.00	4.00	0.09
G. Resident Pa	0.14	0.20	0.33	0.50	2.00	0.33	1.00	1.00	0.33	2.00	0.50	0.04
H. Neighborhoo	0.25	0.25	0.33	0.50	3.03	0.50	1.00	1.00	0.33	2.00	1.00	0.06
I. Negotiated	1.00	0.50	0.50	0.25	4.00	0.50	3.03	3.03	1.00	5.00	6.00	0.15
J. Organizatio	0.50	0.25	0.25	0.33	0.50	0.33	0.50	0.50	0.20	1.00	0.50	0.07
K. Legislation	0.33	0.20	0.33	0.20	3.03	0.25	2.00	1.00	0.17	2.00	1.00	0.11

PRIORITY (HIGH TO LOW) = I B A K D F C J H E G

Player 3 : Land Use & Development Planning
STRATEGIES

	A	B	C	D	E	F	G	H	I	J	K	PRIORITY
A. Attract Bus	1.00	2.00	1.00	1.00	1.00	0.33	1.00	0.33	0.20	1.00	8.00	0.08
B. Employment	0.50	1.00	2.00	1.00	7.00	0.33	0.33	0.11	2.00	1.00	2.00	0.07
C. Minority Bu	1.00	0.50	1.00	0.17	0.17	1.00	4.00	2.00	1.00	1.00	0.20	0.05
D. Comprehensi	1.00	1.00	6.00	1.00	2.00	0.20	0.11	1.00	7.00	1.00	0.20	0.08
E. Utility & I	1.00	0.14	6.00	0.50	1.00	0.17	2.00	7.00	0.17	8.00	0.11	0.09
F. Housing	3.00	3.00	1.00	5.00	6.00	1.00	7.00	8.00	2.00	0.33	1.00	0.15
G. Resident Pa	1.00	3.00	0.25	9.00	0.50	0.14	1.00	0.33	2.00	0.20	0.17	0.06
H. Neighborhoo	3.00	9.00	0.50	1.00	0.14	0.13	3.00	1.00	0.17	4.00	8.00	0.12
I. Negotiated	5.00	0.50	1.00	0.14	6.00	0.50	0.50	6.00	1.00	7.00	0.17	0.11
J. Organizatio	1.00	1.00	1.00	1.00	0.13	3.00	5.00	0.25	0.14	1.00	0.20	0.05
K. Legislation	0.13	0.50	5.00	5.00	9.00	1.00	6.00	0.13	6.00	5.00	1.00	0.14

PRIORITY (HIGH TO LOW) = F K H I E A D B G J C

Player 4 : Community Development
STRATEGIES

	A	B	C	D	E	F	G	H	I	J	K	PRIORITY
A. Attract Bus	1.00	8.00	0.33	0.33	1.00	0.20	4.00	2.00	0.20	4.00	1.00	0.08
B. Employment	0.13	1.00	0.33	0.20	0.17	0.20	0.33	0.17	0.17	0.17	2.00	0.01
C. Minority Bu	3.00	3.00	1.00	0.33	7.00	0.17	0.17	0.33	0.33	4.00	4.00	0.09
D. Comprehensi	3.00	5.00	3.00	1.00	0.11	4.00	1.00	0.20	0.11	0.17	8.00	0.08
E. Utility & I	1.00	6.00	0.14	9.00	1.00	0.17	8.00	1.00	0.17	0.17	0.33	0.08
F. Housing	5.00	5.00	6.00	0.25	6.00	1.00	0.33	0.20	2.00	0.17	0.33	0.09
G. Resident Pa	0.25	3.00	6.00	1.00	0.13	3.00	1.00	0.20	0.33	0.17	0.17	0.05
H. Neighborhoo	0.50	6.00	3.00	5.00	1.00	5.00	5.00	1.00	8.00	7.00	7.00	0.20
I. Negotiated	5.00	6.00	3.00	9.00	6.00	0.50	3.00	0.13	1.00	0.20	4.00	0.12
J. Organizatio	0.25	6.00	0.25	6.00	6.00	6.00	6.00	0.14	5.00	1.00	2.00	0.14
K. Legislation	1.00	0.50	0.25	0.13	3.00	3.00	6.00	0.14	0.25	0.50	1.00	0.06

PRIORITY (HIGH TO LOW) = H J I F C E D A K G B

Figure 6.8. *Preference matrices for development strategies.*

Player 5 : Negotiated Investment Strategy
STRATEGIES

	A	B	C	D	E	F	G	H	I	J	K	PRIORITY
A. Attract Bus	1.00	0.17	0.33	4.00	0.20	0.17	2.00	7.00	0.17	0.17	7.00	0.07
B. Employment	6.00	1.00	0.17	0.33	0.11	0.11	1.00	0.33	2.00	4.00	1.00	0.06
C. Minority Bu	3.00	6.00	1.00	4.00	0.11	2.00	7.00	0.20	8.00	8.00	2.00	0.14
D. Comprehensi	0.25	3.00	0.25	1.00	0.20	4.00	0.20	0.20	0.11	2.00	0.20	0.04
E. Utility & I	5.00	9.00	9.00	5.00	1.00	0.17	8.00	0.17	0.33	0.17	1.00	0.13
F. Housing	6.00	9.00	0.50	0.25	6.00	1.00	0.20	1.00	0.17	2.00	2.00	0.10
G. Resident Pa	0.50	1.00	0.14	5.00	0.13	5.00	1.00	1.00	7.00	2.00	4.00	0.08
H. Neighborhoo	0.14	3.00	5.00	5.00	6.00	1.00	1.00	1.00	7.00	0.11	8.00	0.13
I. Negotiated	6.00	0.50	0.13	9.00	3.00	6.00	0.14	0.14	1.00	0.17	4.00	0.09
J. Organizatio	6.00	0.25	0.13	0.50	6.00	0.50	0.50	9.00	6.00	1.00	0.33	0.13
K. Legislation	0.14	1.00	0.50	5.00	1.00	0.50	0.25	0.13	0.25	3.00	1.00	0.04

PRIORITY (HIGH TO LOW) = C E J H F I G A B K D

Player 6 : Institutional Framework
STRATEGIES

	A	B	C	D	E	F	G	H	I	J	K	PRIORITY
A. Attract Bus	1.00	1.00	4.00	0.33	8.00	0.20	4.00	7.00	7.00	1.00	0.11	0.12
B. Employment	1.00	1.00	1.00	1.00	0.20	0.11	0.20	7.00	0.17	0.17	0.17	0.04
C. Minority Bu	0.25	1.00	1.00	0.11	4.00	7.00	4.00	0.17	4.00	8.00	4.00	0.13
D. Comprehensi	3.00	1.00	9.00	1.00	0.11	0.17	0.20	8.00	1.00	8.00	2.00	0.11
E. Utility & I	0.13	5.00	0.25	9.00	1.00	0.11	8.00	7.00	0.20	2.00	4.00	0.12
F. Housing	5.00	9.00	0.14	6.00	9.00	1.00	0.33	1.00	8.00	7.00	0.33	0.15
G. Resident Pa	0.25	5.00	0.25	5.00	0.13	3.00	1.00	4.00	1.00	1.00	0.20	0.07
H. Neighborhoo	0.14	0.14	6.00	0.13	0.14	1.00	0.25	1.00	1.00	4.00	0.20	0.05
I. Negotiated	0.14	6.00	0.25	1.00	5.00	0.13	1.00	1.00	1.00	7.00	0.17	0.06
J. Organizatio	1.00	6.00	0.13	0.13	0.50	0.14	1.00	0.25	0.14	1.00	1.00	0.03
K. Legislation	9.00	6.00	0.25	0.50	0.25	3.00	5.00	5.00	6.00	1.00	1.00	0.12

PRIORITY (HIGH TO LOW) = F C K E A D G I H B J

Player 7 : Legislative Review
STRATEGIES

	A	B	C	D	E	F	G	H	I	J	K	PRIORITY
A. Attract Bus	1.00	8.00	8.00	0.17	0.33	4.00	0.17	0.17	0.20	1.00	8.00	0.09
B. Employment	0.13	1.00	2.00	0.11	0.11	0.33	0.11	0.11	2.00	8.00	4.00	0.07
C. Minority Bu	0.13	0.50	1.00	8.00	7.00	4.00	1.00	8.00	7.00	0.17	0.17	0.12
D. Comprehensi	6.00	9.00	0.13	1.00	0.20	0.33	4.00	0.17	8.00	0.33	0.20	0.08
E. Utility & I	3.00	9.00	0.14	5.00	1.00	0.20	4.00	0.11	7.00	0.11	4.00	0.09
F. Housing	0.25	3.00	0.25	3.00	5.00	1.00	0.33	1.00	0.20	1.00	4.00	0.06
G. Resident Pa	6.00	9.00	1.00	0.25	0.25	3.00	1.00	1.00	0.17	0.11	2.00	0.07
H. Neighborhoo	6.00	9.00	0.13	6.00	9.00	1.00	1.00	1.00	7.00	0.11	1.00	0.12
I. Negotiated	5.00	0.50	0.14	0.13	0.14	5.00	6.00	0.14	1.00	0.11	7.00	0.06
J. Organizatio	1.00	0.13	6.00	3.00	9.00	1.00	9.00	9.00	9.00	1.00	1.00	0.16
K. Legislation	0.13	0.25	6.00	5.00	0.25	0.25	0.50	1.00	0.14	1.00	1.00	0.06

PRIORITY (HIGH TO LOW) = J H C A E D B G I F K

Player 8 : Public Info & Marketing
STRATEGIES

	A	B	C	D	E	F	G	H	I	J	K	PRIORITY
A. Attract Bus	1.00	0.11	0.17	0.11	0.17	8.00	0.33	0.33	0.11	0.11	0.11	0.03
B. Employment	9.00	1.00	4.00	7.00	8.00	8.00	0.33	0.20	0.20	7.00	0.20	0.12
C. Minority Bu	6.00	0.25	1.00	0.11	0.20	0.11	1.00	0.20	2.00	0.20	7.00	0.06
D. Comprehensi	9.00	0.14	9.00	1.00	8.00	0.17	4.00	0.33	0.33	2.00	7.00	0.11
E. Utility & I	6.00	0.13	5.00	0.13	1.00	0.17	7.00	4.00	0.20	4.00	0.20	0.07
F. Housing	0.13	0.13	9.00	6.00	6.00	1.00	0.33	0.11	0.17	2.00	4.00	0.09
G. Resident Pa	3.00	3.00	1.00	0.25	0.14	3.00	1.00	8.00	0.11	4.00	0.11	0.08
H. Neighborhoo	3.00	5.00	5.00	3.00	0.25	9.00	0.13	1.00	0.20	0.33	7.00	0.12
I. Negotiated	9.00	5.00	0.50	3.00	5.00	6.00	9.00	5.00	1.00	0.33	0.11	0.13
J. Organizatio	9.00	0.14	5.00	0.50	0.25	0.50	0.25	3.00	3.00	1.00	4.00	0.07
K. Legislation	9.00	5.00	0.14	0.14	5.00	0.25	9.00	0.14	9.00	0.25	1.00	0.12

PRIORITY (HIGH TO LOW) = I K B H D F G J E C A

Figure 6.8 (cont'd.)

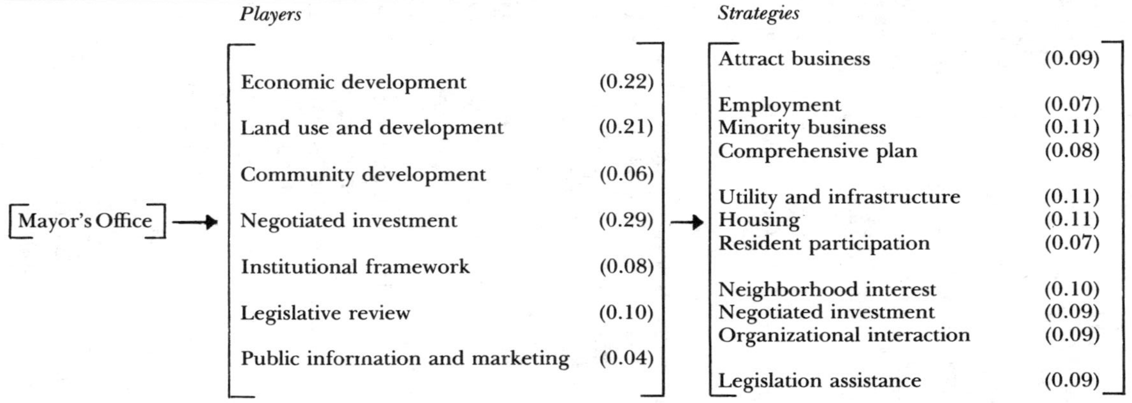

Figure 6.9. *Composite results of priority of strategies.*

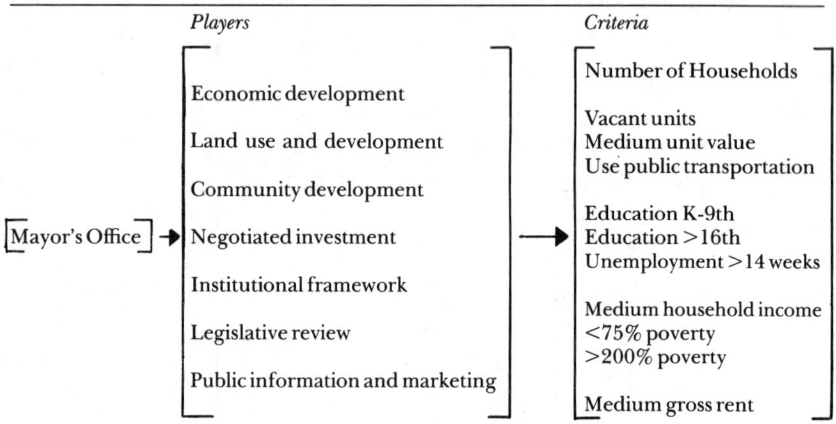

Figure 6.10. *Decision tree number 2—players and evaluation criteria.*

Thematic Mapping

Thematic mapping techniques now can be used to show the location of these census tracts. Figure 6.13 shows the boundaries of all forty-one census tracts in the target area, and the shaded areas represent the priority tracts to be redeveloped. Color can also be used to highlight results. Figure 6.13a presents the first four census tracts rated most comparable; Figure 6.13b shows a second series of five tracts rated next most comparable according to the criteria. From these map outputs, analysts and policy makers can readily locate where resources would be allocated on the basis of the strategies and criteria they select.

The computer-based AHP simulation cannot totally emulate the myriad of choices and bargains that comprise political decisions, particularly as the role of each player is not clear and the issues are not well defined. Neither can we expect that all players will unconditionally accept the preference results aggregated from all players. However, the interactive communication between the player and the computer provides heuristic assistance to lead the player into a logical path when dealing with multi-issue problems. Also, through this hierarchical process, the players can learn how their decisions will affect others and *their* final decisions. The technique can be valuable as a gaming tool to structure an atmosphere of political compromise by illustrating the effects of each player's or coalition's choices on other factors in the process.

The comparables analysis procedure is a quickly implemented selective search routine, ideal for linking preferences or ideas to practical project locations or program recipients. Even without the AHP simula-

Player 1: The Mayor

	A	B	C	D	E	F	G	PRIORITY
A. Economic Development	1.00	2.00	4.00	0.33	2.00	3.00	5.00	0.22
B. Land Use & Development	0.50	1.00	3.00	2.00	3.00	1.00	4.00	0.21
C. Community Development	0.25	0.33	1.00	0.33	0.50	0.50	2.00	0.06
D. Negotiated Investment	3.03	0.50	3.03	1.00	5.00	3.00	7.00	0.29
E. Institional Framework	0.50	0.33	2.00	0.20	1.00	1.00	2.00	0.08
F. Legislative Review	0.33	1.00	2.00	0.33	1.00	1.00	2.00	0.10
G. Public Info & Marketin	0.20	0.25	0.50	0.14	0.50	0.50	1.00	0.04

PRIORITY (HIGH TO LOW) = G C A E D B F

Player 2 : Economic Development
EVALUATION CRITERIA

	A	B	C	D	E	F	G	H	I	J	K	PRIORITY
A. No. Househo	1.00	0.33	2.00	0.11	0.20	0.17	0.20	0.33	7.00	2.00	1.00	0.04
B. Vacant Unit	3.00	1.00	8.00	2.00	0.33	0.11	0.17	2.00	4.00	2.00	0.33	0.07
C. Medium Unit	0.50	0.13	1.00	0.20	0.20	7.00	0.17	7.00	0.33	8.00	0.20	0.08
D. Use Public	9.00	0.50	5.00	1.00	0.33	8.00	0.20	7.00	8.00	0.20	8.00	0.15
E. Education K	5.00	3.00	5.00	3.00	1.00	2.00	0.11	0.20	8.00	0.20	1.00	0.08
F. Education >	6.00	9.00	0.14	0.13	0.50	1.00	4.00	0.20	0.17	8.00	0.33	0.09
G. Unemploymen	5.00	6.00	6.00	5.00	9.00	0.25	1.00	0.11	4.00	8.00	0.17	0.14
H. Medium H.H.	3.00	0.50	0.14	0.14	5.00	5.00	9.00	1.00	0.33	0.17	0.20	0.09
I. <75% Povert	0.14	0.25	3.00	0.13	0.13	6.00	0.25	3.00	1.00	0.17	0.17	0.05
J. >200% Pover	0.50	0.50	0.13	5.00	5.00	0.13	0.13	6.00	6.00	1.00	0.11	0.08
K. Medium Gros	1.00	3.00	5.00	0.13	1.00	3.00	6.00	5.00	6.00	9.00	1.00	0.13

PRIORITY (HIGH TO LOW) = D G K H F J C E B I A

Player 3 : Land Use & Development Planning
EVALUATION CRITERIA

	A	B	C	D	E	F	G	H	I	J	K	PRIORITY
A. No. Househo	1.00	0.17	0.17	0.11	4.00	0.17	8.00	0.33	0.17	1.00	8.00	0.06
B. Vacant Unit	6.00	1.00	0.17	0.17	0.20	7.00	0.33	0.11	0.20	8.00	2.00	0.08
C. Medium Unit	6.00	6.00	1.00	7.00	7.00	0.20	0.33	0.20	0.17	2.00	8.00	0.12
D. Use Public	9.00	6.00	0.14	1.00	2.00	7.00	8.00	7.00	0.17	7.00	2.00	0.15
E. Education K	0.25	5.00	0.14	0.50	1.00	2.00	0.20	2.00	0.33	2.00	8.00	0.06
F. Education >	6.00	0.14	5.00	0.14	0.50	1.00	0.20	0.20	7.00	0.33	4.00	0.09
G. Unemploymen	0.13	3.00	3.00	0.13	5.00	5.00	1.00	2.00	1.00	7.00	0.33	0.09
H. Medium H.H.	3.00	9.00	5.00	0.14	0.50	5.00	0.50	1.00	0.20	1.00	0.11	0.09
I. <75% Povert	6.00	5.00	6.00	6.00	3.00	0.14	1.00	5.00	1.00	0.11	1.00	0.13
J. >200% Pover	1.00	0.13	0.50	0.14	0.50	3.00	0.14	1.00	9.00	1.00	8.00	0.08
K. Medium Gros	0.13	0.50	0.13	0.50	0.13	0.25	3.00	9.00	1.00	0.13	1.00	0.05

PRIORITY (HIGH TO LOW) = D I C G F H J B A E K

Player 4 : Community Development
EVALUATION CRITERIA

	A	B	C	D	E	F	G	H	I	J	K	PRIORITY
A. No. Househo	1.00	7.00	7.00	8.00	0.20	0.11	0.33	4.00	2.00	0.20	2.00	0.09
B. Vacant Unit	0.14	1.00	0.11	7.00	0.11	0.11	8.00	4.00	0.33	2.00	4.00	0.08
C. Medium Unit	0.14	9.00	1.00	1.00	0.33	0.20	8.00	1.00	7.00	0.33	0.20	0.09
D. Use Public	0.13	0.14	1.00	1.00	2.00	0.20	0.33	7.00	0.17	4.00	1.00	0.05
E. Education K	5.00	9.00	3.00	0.50	1.00	8.00	0.20	1.00	0.11	2.00	7.00	0.12
F. Education >	9.00	9.00	5.00	5.00	0.13	1.00	0.17	8.00	1.00	0.20	0.17	0.11
G. Unemploymen	3.00	0.13	0.13	3.00	5.00	6.00	1.00	0.11	7.00	8.00	0.11	0.11
H. Medium H.H.	0.25	0.25	1.00	0.14	1.00	0.13	9.00	1.00	2.00	0.20	7.00	0.08
I. <75% Povert	0.50	3.00	0.14	6.00	9.00	1.00	0.14	0.50	1.00	0.20	8.00	0.09
J. >200% Pover	5.00	0.50	3.00	0.25	0.50	5.00	0.13	5.00	5.00	1.00	7.00	0.10
K. Medium Gros	0.50	0.25	5.00	1.00	0.14	6.00	9.00	0.14	0.13	0.14	1.00	0.08

PRIORITY (HIGH TO LOW) = E G F J C I A K B H D

Figure 6.11. *Preference matrices for evaluation criteria.*

Player 5 : Negotiated Investment Strategy
EVALUATION CRITERIA

	A	B	C	D	E	F	G	H	I	J	K	PRIORITY
A. No. Househo	1.00	0.33	0.11	0.17	7.00	0.17	0.33	0.11	7.00	7.00	2.00	0.08
B. Vacant Unit	3.00	1.00	0.17	2.00	7.00	4.00	0.11	0.33	0.17	0.11	7.00	0.07
C. Medium Unit	9.00	6.00	1.00	4.00	0.20	0.20	0.33	8.00	0.20	8.00	4.00	0.13
D. Use Public	6.00	0.50	0.25	1.00	8.00	0.20	0.11	4.00	8.00	8.00	0.20	0.11
E. Education K	0.14	0.14	5.00	0.13	1.00	2.00	2.00	0.33	0.33	0.11	0.11	0.04
F. Education >	6.00	0.25	5.00	5.00	0.50	1.00	1.00	2.00	4.00	0.17	2.00	0.09
G. Unemploymen	3.00	9.00	3.00	9.00	0.50	1.00	1.00	1.00	0.33	0.20	7.00	0.11
H. Medium H.H.	9.00	3.00	0.13	0.25	3.00	0.50	1.00	1.00	0.17	8.00	0.11	0.08
I. <75% Povert	0.14	6.00	5.00	0.13	3.00	0.25	3.00	6.00	1.00	8.00	0.17	0.11
J. >200% Pover	0.14	9.00	0.13	0.13	9.00	6.00	5.00	0.13	0.13	1.00	8.00	0.11
K. Medium Gros	0.50	0.14	0.25	5.00	9.00	0.50	0.14	9.00	6.00	0.13	1.00	0.09

PRIORITY (HIGH TO LOW) = C G D J I F K H A B E

Player 6 : Institutional Framework
EVALUATION CRITERIA

	A	B	C	D	E	F	G	H	I	J	K	PRIORITY
A. No. Househo	1.00	2.00	4.00	1.00	8.00	0.20	0.17	0.17	0.33	0.33	0.20	0.05
B. Vacant Unit	0.50	1.00	2.00	8.00	8.00	2.00	0.17	1.00	4.00	0.17	0.20	0.09
C. Medium Unit	0.25	0.50	1.00	0.20	4.00	0.11	8.00	7.00	1.00	2.00	4.00	0.10
D. Use Public	1.00	0.13	5.00	1.00	0.33	7.00	4.00	1.00	0.17	7.00	0.17	0.10
E. Education K	0.13	0.13	0.25	3.00	1.00	0.20	0.20	4.00	0.11	0.17	4.00	0.05
F. Education >	5.00	0.50	9.00	0.14	5.00	1.00	0.11	0.20	2.00	0.11	7.00	0.10
G. Unemploymen	6.00	6.00	0.13	0.25	5.00	9.00	1.00	4.00	1.00	0.20	2.00	0.11
H. Medium H.H.	6.00	1.00	0.14	1.00	0.25	5.00	0.25	1.00	4.00	1.00	8.00	0.09
I. <75% Povert	3.00	0.25	1.00	6.00	9.00	0.50	1.00	0.25	1.00	4.00	8.00	0.11
J. >200% Pover	3.00	6.00	0.50	0.14	6.00	9.00	5.00	1.00	0.25	1.00	0.11	0.10
K. Medium Gros	5.00	5.00	0.25	6.00	0.25	0.14	0.50	0.13	0.13	9.00	1.00	0.10

PRIORITY (HIGH TO LOW) = I G J D C F K H B A E

Player 7 : Legislative Review
EVALUATION CRITERIA

	A	B	C	D	E	F	G	H	I	J	K	PRIORITY
A. No. Househo	1.00	4.00	8.00	7.00	0.20	8.00	8.00	2.00	7.00	7.00	0.17	0.16
B. Vacant Unit	0.25	1.00	1.00	2.00	0.20	0.20	0.17	8.00	7.00	8.00	8.00	0.09
C. Medium Unit	0.13	1.00	1.00	0.20	2.00	0.11	7.00	8.00	2.00	2.00	0.20	0.07
D. Use Public	0.14	0.50	5.00	1.00	8.00	4.00	7.00	1.00	0.33	4.00	0.11	0.10
E. Education K	5.00	5.00	0.50	0.13	1.00	0.17	0.11	7.00	2.00	2.00	0.17	0.07
F. Education >	0.13	5.00	9.00	0.25	6.00	1.00	0.11	7.00	7.00	1.00	7.00	0.12
G. Unemploymen	0.13	6.00	0.14	0.14	9.00	9.00	1.00	0.11	4.00	0.33	4.00	0.12
H. Medium H.H.	0.50	0.13	0.13	1.00	0.14	0.14	9.00	1.00	1.00	0.33	0.11	0.05
I. <75% Povert	0.14	0.14	0.50	3.00	0.50	0.14	0.25	1.00	1.00	7.00	4.00	0.05
J. >200% Pover	0.14	0.13	0.50	0.25	0.50	1.00	3.00	3.00	0.14	1.00	4.00	0.05
K. Medium Gros	6.00	0.13	5.00	9.00	6.00	0.14	0.25	9.00	0.25	0.25	1.00	0.12

PRIORITY (HIGH TO LOW) = A K F G D B E C H I J

Player 8 : Public Info & Marketing
EVALUATION CRITERIA

	A	B	C	D	E	F	G	H	I	J	K	PRIORITY
A. No. Househo	1.00	8.00	1.00	4.00	8.00	0.11	0.33	2.00	0.17	8.00	0.17	0.12
B. Vacant Unit	0.13	1.00	2.00	7.00	0.20	0.11	7.00	4.00	7.00	0.20	1.00	0.09
C. Medium Unit	1.00	0.50	1.00	7.00	0.33	2.00	0.20	0.20	1.00	0.33	0.20	0.05
D. Use Public	0.25	0.14	0.14	1.00	1.00	7.00	4.00	2.00	0.33	2.00	0.33	0.08
E. Education K	0.13	5.00	3.00	1.00	1.00	8.00	4.00	0.33	0.33	0.11	0.33	0.09
F. Education >	9.00	9.00	0.50	0.14	0.13	1.00	7.00	2.00	7.00	2.00	4.00	0.15
G. Unemploymen	3.00	0.14	5.00	0.25	0.25	0.14	1.00	0.33	0.20	0.11	2.00	0.04
H. Medium H.H.	0.50	0.25	5.00	0.50	3.00	0.50	3.00	1.00	4.00	7.00	8.00	0.10
I. <75% Povert	6.00	0.14	1.00	3.00	3.00	0.14	5.00	0.25	1.00	7.00	8.00	0.11
J. >200% Pover	0.13	5.00	3.00	0.50	9.00	0.50	9.00	0.14	0.14	1.00	4.00	0.09
K. Medium Gros	6.00	1.00	5.00	3.00	3.00	0.25	0.50	0.13	0.13	0.25	1.00	0.07

PRIORITY (HIGH TO LOW) = F A I H B J E D K C G

Figure 6.11. (cont'd.)

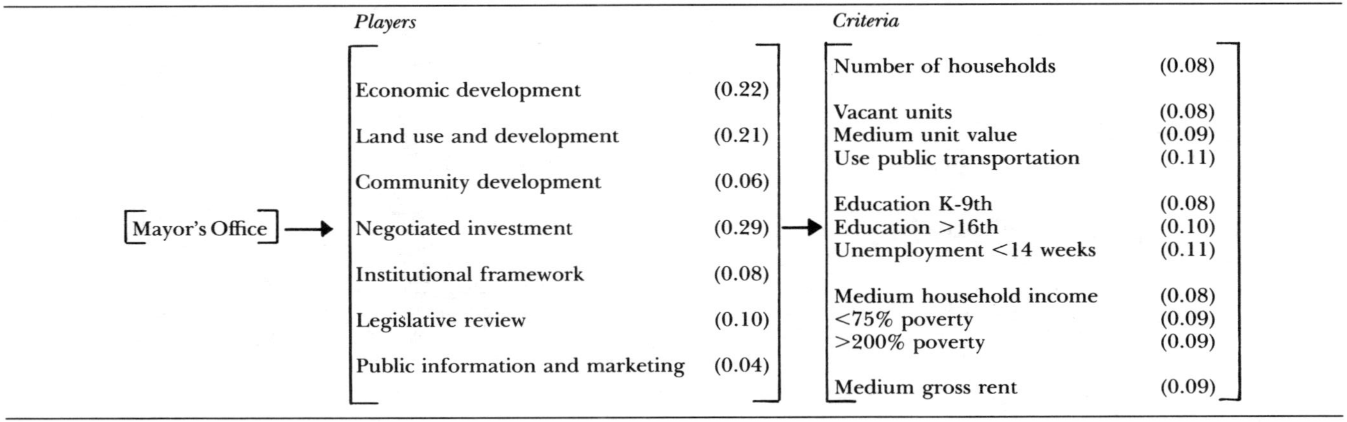

Figure 6.12. *Composite results of priority of evaluation criteria.*

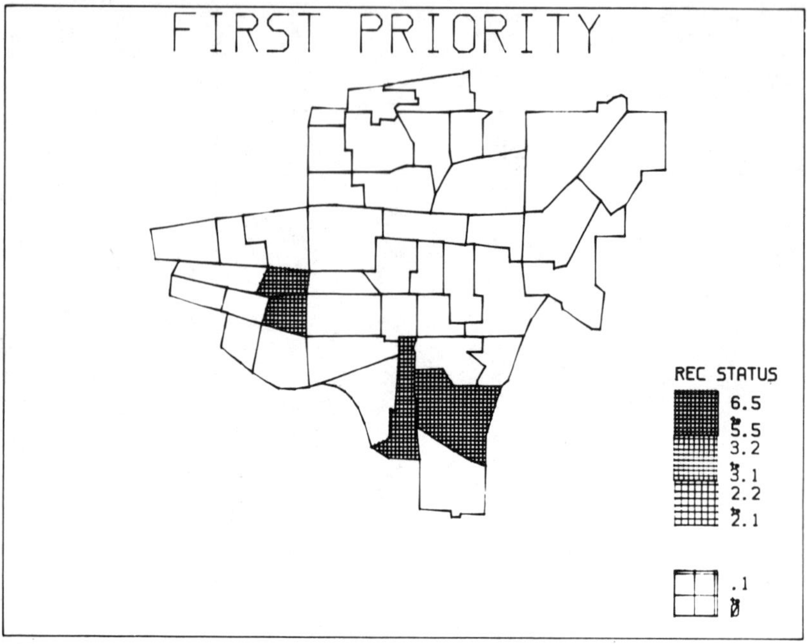

Figure 6.13a. *Top priority census tracts selected by weighted criteria.*

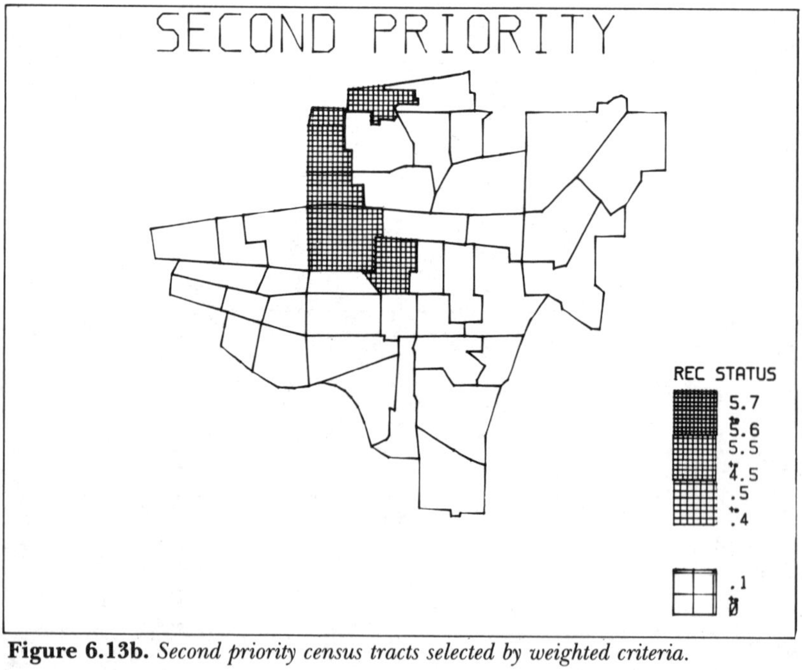

Figure 6.13b. *Second priority census tracts selected by weighted criteria.*

tion it can be used effectively in a planning department and in fact is frequently so used in Cleveland. Finally, thematic mapping routines help communicate spatial data more strongly by appealing to our considerable capacity for processing visual information.

In summary, the microcomputer applied to geoprocessing is an inexpensive, self-paced educational tool that can help managers learn state-of-the-art techniques to improve productivity in the planning field. Most systems supported by microcomputers will improve the efficiency of planners' conventional work and will lead them to discover new applications. In other words, planners using these new tools can not only iteratively build experience but also apply their experience creatively to extend their knowledge.

References

Baxter, Richard S. 1976. *Computer and Statistical Techniques for Planners.* London: Methuen.

Chasen, Sylvan H. 1978. *Geometric Principles and Procedures for Computer Graphic Applications.* Englewood Cliffs, N.J.: Prentice-Hall.

Costello, M., and L. Garvin. 1982. "A Map-Based Information System to Support Reappraisal." In *48th International Conference on Assessment Administration.* Chicago: International Association of Assessing Officers.

Darin-Drabkin, Haim. 1977. *Land Policy and Urban Growth.* Elmsford, N.Y.: Pergamon Press.

Foley, James D., and Andries Van Dam. 1982. *Fundamentals of Interactive Computer Graphics.* Reading, Mass.: Addison-Wesley.

Goldberg, M., and P. Chinloy. 1984. *Urban Land Economics.* New York: John Wiley.

Haben, Ralph Norman. 1983. "Stimulus Information and Processing Mechanisms in Visual Space Perception." In *Human and Machine Vision,* edited by Jacob Beck *et al.* New York: Academic Press.

Lam, H.S.A. 1984. "Geographic Information Systems (GIS) and Spatial Analyses in Microcomputers." In *The Changing Role of Computers in Public Agencies.* Washington, D.C.: Urban and Regional Information Systems Association.

———. 1985. "Microcomputer Mapping for Local Governments." In *Auto Carto 7: International Symposium of Computer Assisted Cartography.* Washington, D.C.: ASP/ACSM.

Larson, Richard C., and Amedeo R. Odoni. 1981. *Urban Operations Research.* Englewood Cliffs, N.J.: Prentice-Hall.

Monmonier, Mark S. 1982. *Computer-Assisted Cartography: Principles and Prospects.* Englewood Cliffs, N.J.: Prentice-Hall.

National Research Council (U.S.). 1982. *Modernization of the Public Land Survey System.* Washington, D.C.: National Academy Press.

———. 1983. "Panel on a Multipurpose Cadastre." In *Procedures and Standards for a Multipurpose Cadastre.* Washington, D.C.: National Academy Press.

Peucker, T.K. 1972. *Computer Cartography.* Washington, D.C.: Association of American Geographers.

Slater, David C. 1984. *Management of Local Planning.* Washington, D.C.: International City Management Association.

Smith, Dennis R., Gary R. Smith, and Catherine M. Coffey. 1982. "Land Use Suitability Mapping. In *Computer Graphic World.* San Francisco: Computer Graphic World Publishing.

U.S. Department of Commerce, Bureau of the Census. 1980. "State and Local Ratio Studies, Property Tax Assessment, and Transfer Taxes." In *State and Local Government Special Studies No. 99.* Washington, D.C.: U.S. Government Printing Office.

U.S. Department of Transportation, Federal Highway Administration. 1977. *PLANPAC/BACKPAC General Information Manual.* Washington, D.C.: U.S. Government Printing Office.

7

Network Analysis

Jan Schreiber

The steadily increasing sophistication of microcomputers in graphic representation and their parallel increases in memory and disk storage capacity make them more and more capable of solving geospatial problems for planners in a way that offers clear advantages over earlier methods. In particular, microcomputers can now perform many tasks related to network analysis that used to be possible only on the powerful but less flexible time-shared mainframe computer.

Networks and Polygons

To place network analysis in a context, it is useful to distinguish networks conceptually and functionally from other graphic entities. The most fundamental entity is the point, which has location but no dimension. In microcomputer graphic systems, points are located on an implied two-dimensional plane oriented by coordinates in horizontal (X) and vertical (Y) directions. Thus two numbers must be stored in the computer's memory for every point recorded, not to mention special identifying labels that may be numbers, letters, or entire words. The more complex the shape to be recorded, the more points must be stored; thus complex shapes, even if small in area, place greater loads on a computer's storage capacity than simple ones.

Lines are represented by linking two points. To link one point to another means to add to its representation in computer storage an identifier of a second point. A series of points may be joined together in a linked list; the result, called a chain, is a series of line segments joined end-to-end. Should the endpoint of the chain be linked to its beginning point, the result is a polygon, which of course can approximate a physical area and thus function as a map. The more points one uses (and thus the more computer storage), the greater the accuracy of the approximation.

However, the purpose of drawing lines may be not to enclose space but simply to connect many points together—not necessarily all in series like the stops on a bus route, but in a set of complex relationships like the interstices of a spiderweb. The result is a network, a spatial configuration in which areas are irrelevant but distances (however defined) and connectivity govern all the relationships. The primary units in networks are links (line segments) and nodes (the points at which line segments are joined). A sufficient specification of a network is one that indicates, for each node, the nodes to which it is directly linked and the length of the link. In addition, it is possible to treat networks as directed or undirected. In the latter type, movement along a link is considered to be possible in either direction; in the former, movement is possible in one direction only.

For a given configuration of nodes, any associated link lengths and pattern of directions are possible, even though only some can exist in a Euclidean world governed by the rules of standard geometry. This makes it possible to store on a computer disk connectivity information (what is linked to what) for a set of nodes, followed by several different possible sets of link lengths and directional values. (See Table 7.1.) The usefulness of maintaining several such sets will become clear later in this discussion.

Table 7.1
Portion of a Network as Stored in Computer Memory

		Link Values		
Node	*Linked to*	*(Type 1)*	*(Type 2)*	*(Type 3)*
A	B	5.0	5.0	57
	E	7.1	7.1	84
	F	6.3	−6.3	23
	G	3.3	−3.3	12
B	A	5.0	−5.0	57
	C	3.1	3.1	36
	F	2.2	−2.2	41
C	B	3.1	−3.1	36
	F	5.2	5.2	75
	G	4.5	4.5	49
	I	9.0	−9.0	60
...	...	...	...	...

Some Sample Applications

Because all these relationships can be represented digitally (graphic portrayal is a desirable but not necessary adjunct), the computer is well suited to analyze networks. The applications in an urban setting are numerous. Broadly, they comprise transport, communications, services, and utilities.

Transport applications generally involve shortest-path computations, or the determination of the shortest distances from each point to every other point. This category includes a wide range of problems such as street layout, traffic flow design, subway route planning, and the like.

Communications applications involve the layout of telephone lines, television cables, and, within more restricted areas, cables connecting microcomputers into a local area network. Since these problems do not involve a vehicle going out from a depot, covering all points along a path, and returning to its source, the concept of a route is not relevant. (Signals sent along wires are routed, of course, but because their propagation time is infinitesimal, it is not usually helpful to compare several routings.) What is most useful for communications problems is the notion of the minimum spanning tree: a configuration of links that connect all nodes in the network such that their aggregate net distance is smallest. (See Figure 7.1.)

Services, such as police, fire, garbage collection, and mail delivery, fall into two broad classes. Some involve movement of vehicles from a central node (such as a police station) to any one of a large number of other nodes within the network. It is important to know the shortest route from this base node to each other node. Other services require that each point along the route (link points as well as nodes) be covered each time a vehicle goes out. (See Figure 7.2.) Garbage collection and mail delivery fall into this class. Such problems are known as edge-covering problems; they employ different algorithms than those involving shortest-path communications, and they differ from minimum spanning tree problems in that they must ensure coverage of *all* links, not just those needed to connect all nodes.

Finally, *utilities* such as water and sewage systems usually share with communications the need to connect every node of a network into a single linkage as efficiently as possible. In such cases they also employ the minimum spanning tree algorithms. However, if connections must be considered to all points along a straight line, not just to nodal points (again, see Figure 7.2), edgecovering algorithms of a kind collectively known as the traveling salesman's path may be appropriate.

The choice of the appropriate computational approach for a given problem is dictated largely by the specific configurations involved and

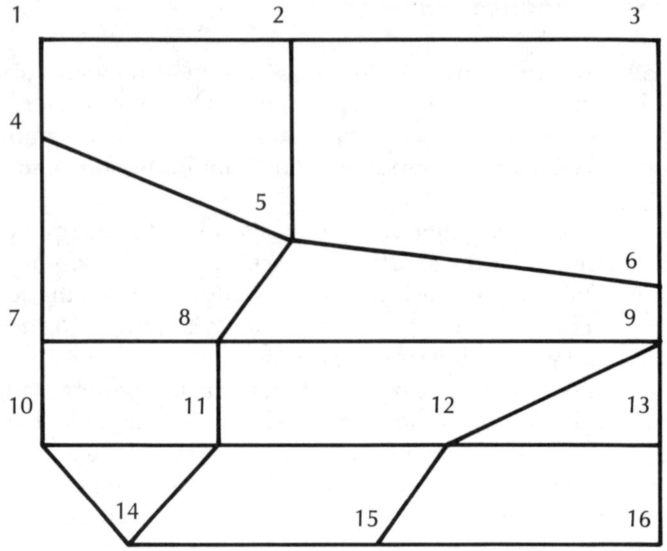

MINIMUM SPANNING TREE L = 415

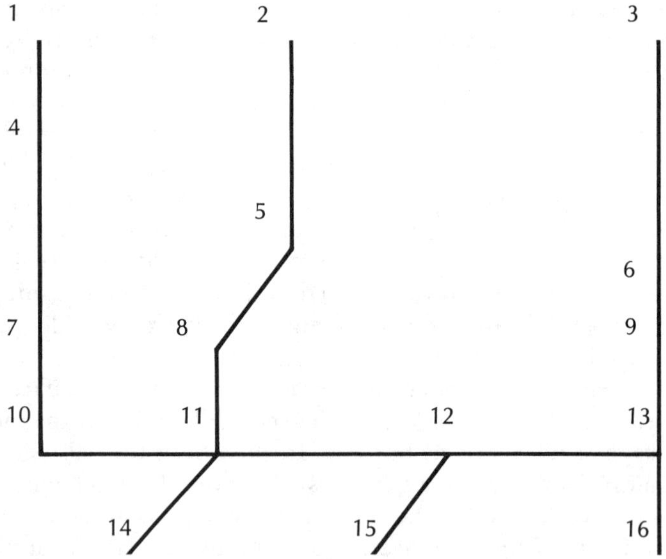

Figure 7.1. *A network (top) with its minimum spanning tree. (Total length of the links needed to connect all nodes is 415 units.)*

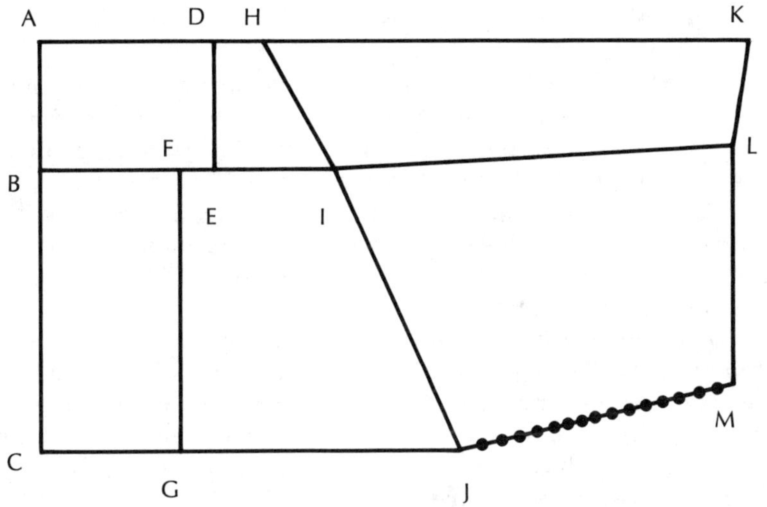

Figure 7.2. *A network with nodes at A, B, C, D, E, F, G, H, I, J, K, L, M.* (*Points between J and M, which might be houses along a street, are not nodes; if coverage of them is important, then an edge-covering algorithm is needed.*)

whether only nodes or all the points along a link are to be taken into account. The most useful computer programs for such problems are the most generic ones—those that offer the user a menu of general algorithms, each of which may be applied to the problem at hand. (See Table 7.2.) In the next section we shall also adopt a generic approach and consider each of the major network algorithms in itself, with only passing reference to their possible applications.

Table 7.2
Type of Network Analysis Applicable to Typical Planning Problems

	Shortest Path				
Planning application	*One node to all nodes*	*Each node to each other*	*Minimum spanning tree*	*Node covering (traveling salesman's path)*	*Edge covering (Chinese postman's problem)*
Transport	x	x			
Communications			x		
Services	x				x
Utilities			x	x	

The Major Network Algorithms

The simplest algorithm is that used to compute the minimum spanning tree. From any node used as a starting point (since all nodes must ultimately be included), one finds the shortest link to another node. From this second node one looks for the shortest link again, excluding the one already used in coming from the first node. One continues in this fashion until all the nodes are connected. The result will be a subset of the links in the network. The total of their lengths is the length of the minimum spanning tree.

Two observations that we can make here apply to all the other algorithms as well. The first is that if a variety of link lengths are available to the computer, depending on the *type* of link being examined, then the configuration (and of course also the total length) of the minimum spanning tree may change from type to type, even though the connectivity of the network itself remains unchanged.

The second, related, observation is that links do not have to be measured exclusively in terms of *distance.* It is quite possible, for example, to make the link values equal to the time required to traverse a given distance, rather than the distance itself. Since transit time may be affected by such things as terrain (or road condition), traffic density, or available mode of travel, a network may well exist in which the time required to get from one node to a node on its opposite side is shorter than the time required to go to an adjacent node. Certain edgecovering and nodecovering algorithms will produce odd-appearing results when non-Euclidean link values are involved—for example, a value for the hypotenuse of a triangle that is not the square root of the sum of the squares of its two sides.

As indicated previously, two kinds of shortest-path algorithms are available, depending on the user's need. The first and more rapid one is useful in cases when all trips have the same starting point—for example, when a fire department must be prepared to get to any street corner in a city precinct by the shortest possible route. The shortest path to the nearest node is computed first, then the shortest path from that node to the next nearest (such that the total distance is as small as possible), and so on until all nodes have been accounted for. Distance is tallied in each case as well. On conclusion of the algorithm, the computer has in memory a list of all nodes and, for each of them, the previous node in the path from the base node and the distance involved. When the user requests the distance from the base node to some other node, the program starts with the destination node and works backward, through the various previous nodes (keeping track of total distance as it goes along), till it comes to the base node. It then prints out the path in proper order and the distance.

If the program is capable of producing numerical information only, the path will be given in the form of a series of node identifiers, thus:

12 2 21 16 4 18 15

However, if the program is capable of producing graphic images on screen or paper, the computer screen may present an image of the entire network, then show in a different color the shortest paths from the base node to all other nodes. Since these images can be produced as the computations are being made, the effect of seeing sections of a network progressively colored in as they become part of the shortest path is often dramatic.

The more complete shortest-path algorithm is invoked when it is advantageous to have in the computer's memory at one time a basis for finding instantly the shortest path between any two points in the network. One need not start from a base node (such as a depot or station) but might start anywhere and go to anywhere else, like a taxicab. In solving this problem the computer creates in memory a matrix resembling the table found in some road maps, in which one can find the shortest distance between any two cities. A parallel matrix contains in each cell the previous node in a path *from* any node *to* any node. By starting with the destination node and running through the information in this table until the "previous" node turns out to be the starting node, the computer can quickly construct the path and display it numerically.

The disadvantage of this routine is the large amount of memory it consumes and the length of time it takes to perform the matrix computations. As it happens, computation time increases with the cube of the number of nodes involved. On the other hand, compiled programs working on modern 16- and 32-bit microcomputers are sufficiently fast that this limitation does not become problematic until quite a large number of nodes are used.

Like the previous routine, this one can be used to drive a graphic display in which the entire network is pictured. When the user asks the computer to show a shortest path between two nodes, the path is immediately outlined in a different color, and the distance involved is shown numerically. As soon as the question is asked again using a second pair of nodes, the first colored path is erased, and a second is depicted.

Such graphic representations can be extremely useful in illustrating how a shortest path changes with different assumptions about traveling times between the network nodes. It can and does happen that during rush-hour traffic conditions, the shortest route in time is more than twice the length of the shortest route in distance. Drivers tend to discover such things unsystematically on their own. It would even be possible to model the effect of widespread use of computer-based shortest-path algorithms, on the assumption that drivers might alter their customary routes in response to such knowledge, thereby changing congestion patterns.

The logical extension of these shortest-path problems is a classic known as the traveling salesman's tour. In the form that is easiest to solve, it assumes a fully connected network—that is, one in which every node is directly linked to every other node. Given such linkage, the question then is: what is the shortest tour[1] that covers all nodes and returns to the starting point? A fully connected network is a rarity, but it can be approximated mathematically by first performing the second of the shortest-path routines discussed above. This places in the computer's memory a matrix containing, for every node, the distance to every other, even though in some cases the trip may be via intermediate nodes. On the basis of this matrix the computer can now calculate the order of visits to the nodes such that the cumulative distance traveled is minimized.

Unless the network is fully connected, some of the connections shown in the resulting path will not be between adjacent nodes. In such cases the user is to assume that the distant node is reached by the shortest path given in the previous routine. The algorithm used in this solution involves a complex process of testing elements of a matrix and shifting cell entries about until all tests are met. On microcomputers using programs in interpreted languages, it can be quite time consuming for larger numbers of nodes.

The solution to this problem can also be expressed graphically, with the traveling salesman's tour traced in color on the computer screen, or plotted or printed as the user instructs.

So far we have discussed node-to-node problems, which are of greatest use to network analysis in cases where only the interstices of the network are of interest. (Sometimes, of course, this is simply a convenient fiction. Police dispatchers tend to orient themselves and their detectives by means of street corners—Hollywood and Vine, Broadway and 33rd—even though the ultimate destination may be halfway down the block. But in practical terms we are not far off if we figure shortest paths on a node-to-node basis.) But sometimes what matters is not that every node be covered per se, but rather that every link be traversed. If that is the case, we are dealing with an edge-covering problem.

The most venerable edge-covering problem relates to what is called the Euler tour, after the Swiss mathematician Leonard Euler. Legend has it that in the 1730s Euler was given the problem of planning a route for a town parade in the Russian city of Koenigsberg, which had seven bridges. Euler was asked to ensure that the parade would cross every bridge only once before returning to its starting point. The problem as

[1]In mathematical usage applied to problems like these, a path is any route of travel from one point to another; a tour returns to its starting point.

posed proved impossible for the town in question, but Euler discovered how to analyze a network to determine whether such a tour were feasible. Today the analysis can be done quickly by computer, using Euler's method. If an Euler tour (as it now is called) is impossible, we can nevertheless determine which streets (links) must be traversed more than once to return to the starting point with the minimum distance covered in traversing all links.

The general problem is called the Chinese postman's problem, and indeed the algorithm is a useful one in determining optimum postal delivery systems, and not just in China. (Its name comes from the fact that it was first published in the *Chinese Journal of Mathematics.)* What Euler discovered in his search for a parade route was that nodes with an odd number of links are the bugbear. If you are a postal carrier determined to minimize your labor, you will have no problem if you can come to a street corner and leave again by a different road, but if you return to the same corner by a third road and find there is no way out that hasn't already been walked before, you are stuck. If there are only two such odd-degree nodes, you can start at one and end at the other and have an Euler path (that is, a route that ends in a different place from its starting point but still covers all links). But if you want to produce an Euler tour (where the starting and ending points are in the same place), there can be no nodes of odd degree. Usually, therefore, a solution to the Chinese postman's problem involves adding just enough links (repeating paths) to nodes of odd degree to produce an Euler path. The object is to choose the links to be repeated such that the shortest net distance is added.

Computer procedures for this operation are different from those a person would use in tracing the path with a pencil, and indeed, the computer solution can be quite complex, though not inordinately time-consuming. Graphic representations of the solution are not as helpful as in the other cases, since *all* the links will be covered and the resulting figure does not differ (except in that some links are used twice) from the network itself. The most useful output is a list of links in the order they are to be covered, with the extra links emphasized, along with the total length.

Some Limitations

Microcomputers are fairly new to this kind of work. In the past they lacked sufficient disk storage and random access memory to make the processing of very large networks feasible. Furthermore—and this is still a problem for some personal computers—they operated slowly.

Speeds measured in milliseconds may not seem slow, but when the iterations must be repeated millions of times, the operating speed of hardware can clearly be a limiting factor.

For this reason computer scientists and programmers have attempted to develop measures of algorithmic complexity that convey an idea of the time required for operation. Such measures must be approximate, of course, since programmers cannot know in advance how many nodes an algorithm will have to cope with or how many links per node. But in general, for algorithms involving polynomial computations, the slowness of computation will be determined by the order of the highest power to which the polynomial is raised. Thus, a polynomial whose highest term is raised to the third power will represent a significantly longer computation time than one whose highest term is only squared. In developing computer programs to analyze networks, programmers have tended to steer clear of potentially time consuming algorithms, sometimes at the expense of offering inexact heuristic solutions because they will run more quickly.

However, three forces are working to reduce processing times in general and bring practical network analysis within the ambit of the microcomputer. The first is the advent of the fixed disk drive system. Input/output operations with such disks are significantly faster than with floppy disks; as a result, information can be loaded into memory much more rapidly. This is particularly important in the case of very large data bases that exceed the capacity of memory for storage and thus must be brought into memory on a piecemeal basis.

The second force is faster microprocessors. Sixteen- and 32-bit processors are becoming increasingly common and are starting to dominate the personal computer field. More complex chip architecture is being developed, permitting a wider range of capabilities and more rapid computation than in the past. The notable difference in processing speed between the IBM PC/XT and the PC/AT illustrates these developments, and the AT by no means represents the pinnacle.

Thirdly, there is a movement from interpreted to compiled programs. The language in which many microcomputer programs were first developed was interpreted BASIC, a versatile language but slow because each line had to be translated into machine code every time it was encountered. Since network analysis typically involves repetitive loops, as we have seen, the drag on efficiency using programs written in this language was significant. Compiled languages, by contrast, produce machine code once and for all as they are written; operations carried out in such languages typically run from twenty to thirty times faster. Moreover, compiled programs have access to much more of the computer's total memory than do interpreted programs, and as a result more information can be stored in active memory at one time.

In short, there is less and less reason to regard network processing on the microcomputer as a curiosity but not a practical option. It is true that some time must be consumed in entering the data in the first place, but this time would have to be spent with any computer, and the advantages of speed and accuracy of processing once data entry is complete are usually decisive. Furthermore, more and more microcomputer programs are available allowing users to download and use geographic data from large computers. Given the improved graphic capabilities of today's micros, which make the presentation and interpretation of spatial data almost simultaneous processes, they are rapidly becoming a realistic tool for use with such tasks as traffic management, communications design, transit system planning, and the laying out of city service networks.

Modeling with Network Programs

So far we have discussed networks as if they were fixed collections of data reflecting concrete situations in the real world. They often are. But there are numerous occasions when it is in a planner's interest to construct a number of hypothetical models and pursue the consequences of each. One of the chief values of network analysis lies in the ability to do just that, though individual programs vary in the extent to which they facilitate modeling. Here we will discuss a number of approaches to modeling, which will vary in ease or cumbersomeness depending on the particular program used.

The simplest means of testing alternative models is to provide for a given network configuration several different values of links. The computer, of course, is neutral as to the units assigned to link values. Some may be units of distance, some units of time, and some more complex units such as "average pound-miles," which might be used to approximate the subjective distance of a letter carrier's route. If the computer program permits the user to store on disk a number of values for any given link, then any chosen set of values can be read and used in a particular analysis, and the results of using each set can be compared. In this way an optimum solution can be identified, or several solutions can be recommended depending on exogenous conditions such as time of day or weather conditions.

Related to this process, directed link values can be stored alongside nondirected ones. The difference is frequently only a change of sign. (One convention is to assign negative distance values to links on which one may not move from a subject node to a next node.) The program can then be instructed to treat the network as nondirected, in which case the absolute value of each link is used in computation, or as directed. Shortest-path algorithms that take account of direction will then show a different path between nodes *A* and *B* than between nodes *B* and *A*. In this way one can experiment with two or more arrangements of one-way and two-way streets in a section of a city and identify the shortest paths between key nodes that will result from each arrangement.

Even more flexibility is given (though not all programs permit this) when the user need not enter for disk storage the structure and link values of every network he wants to analyze. If a program has sufficient memory available to it, the capability of accepting a network of any desired structure directly from the keyboard greatly enhances its value as a modeling tool. In such a case the user need not have anticipated all possible relevant network structures or sets of link values when the original network was entered and stored on disk; he can instead record an ad hoc idea or hunch and test its consequences for communications, service delivery, or what have you. Ideally, models created in this way can be subsequently stored on disk if they prove valuable in comparative analysis.

Some Larger Views

The distinction between strategic and tactical planning sounds useful and is often made—to the subtle denigration of the tactical. But in practice it is frequently difficult to identify which is which. It is of course possible to take a progressively larger view of any subject, seeing it in wider and wider contexts, with each new view seeming a strategic perspective and leaving the previous ones, by default, with the label *tactical.* The analysis of urban environments, including network analysis, can readily be discussed in such terms. It is wise, however, to avoid concluding that the bigger the network (or the more parcels) one is capable of analyzing, the more nearly the analysis becomes a strategic planning tool. Strategic planning, if that overused term has any meaning, connotes not just a quantitative but a qualitative difference in approach. Not only must one know the shortest paths between all points in a given network, for example, but one must also know what developments in transportation are around the corner, what the economic expectations for the city's downtown area are over the next decade, what political (as well as experiential) motivations lie behind recent complaints about city service delivery, what economic and other relations can be expected between local, state, and federal levels of government, and a host of other facts and feelings, some measurable, some inferable, and others likely to remain mysterious.

So it should be understood that network analysis, like any other analytic approach, is essentially a tactical or operational tool. Analyzing larger networks will not necessarily help us to see the bigger picture. This point is made to encourage the use of this analytic tool even if the available hardware or software will permit only relatively small networks to be examined. The habit of modeling by computer is valuable, even if the models are of necessity small. And they need not be extremely small. Current microcomputer software can readily permit analysis of a network of a hundred nodes and an average of five links per node. A hundred street corners comprise a sizable portion of a city. Very soon it will be possible to do more than that, to encompass all nodes of even a large city in a microcomputer database. But it is good to remember that smaller areas are actually more useful for modeling than larger ones, in that the variables to be adjusted are more manageable. Even a modest network analysis capability can be an excellent planning tool.

As yet, planners do not have a wide range of choice in the matter of software. Since network programs have application only in limited fields (in contrast to, say, spreadsheet programs), large, commercial software houses do not offer them. Small developers who create them for their own use are not able to publicize their work readily, and in any case their programs are often tied to idiosyncratic data base structures that are incompatible with other systems a user may have at hand. (See Table 6.2 in the previous chapter for a partial list of geographic analysis programs.) With these facts in mind, some researchers (see Larson and Odoni 1981 and Goodchild and Noronha 1983) have simply published algorithms, which can be realized by planners with some programming ability, on the computer (and in the language) of their choice.

The Lincoln Institute, as part of its SOLIR land data system software, has included a network capability that works on data stored in the same manner as all other data in the system. Prototype modifications of these modules display the network, with labeled nodes, on the graphic computer screen and highlight shortest paths in a second color. The system works well, and other network processors have also been released by smaller private vendors; but it should be noted that all such systems are in early stages of development. They can be used as working tools and will give good results, but the developers are still open to suggestions for enhancement and extension of their capabilities. Users who decide to augment their own analytic power with such tools at this point can also have the satisfaction of contributing to their ultimate form and range.

References

Goodchild, Michael F., and Valerian T. Noronha. 1983. "Location-Allocation for Small Computers." Department of Geography, University of Western Ontario (unpublished).

Larson, Richard C., and Amedeo R. Odoni. 1981. *Urban Operations Research.* Englewood Cliffs, N.J.: Prentice-Hall.

8

Planning the New Planning Office

Mathew E. MacIver

The preceding chapters have indicated general ideas where the work of local government can be facilitated or improved with the judicious use of microcomputer technology, used as tools for both communication and computation. These general precepts, in fact, can be used as the basis for developing policy regarding the use of computer assisted methods. But policy is only as timely and accurate, and thus as effective, as the means with which it can be implemented. Hence, it is wise to find ways of evaluating the costs and benefits of alternative system design choices. As in other policy matters, planning for implementation requires both quantitative and anecdotal analysis.

Benefit/Cost Analysis

The technique of benefit/cost analysis has become ever more popular since its ascendance to orthodox government practice in the Department of Defense some twenty years ago. Two of the projects on which I have used the technique will help to indicate the breadth of its applicability. On one occasion, there was a need to evaluate the effects of government loan subsidies on office development in the United States; on another occasion, cost/benefit analysis was used to compare the overall effects of different government medical interventions on mortality and morbidity caused by an insidious tropical disease. The execution of the method is simple, given a knowledge of discounting and simple arithmetic. The difficult part is, first, defining the scope of the analysis and, second, assigning quantifiable weights to costs and benefits that are not accurately priced on the open market. The first project cited above was relatively well defined in both of these areas, but the second was more slippery because the number of beneficiaries was difficult to estimate and, more important, the benefits of preserving human life could not be satisfactorily quantified.

Although decisions regarding information systems are rarely a matter of life and death, the structure of the analysis in the case of planning applications is closer to the latter example. Even though we know that the point of all information systems is to improve communication, does this mean that an evaluation of a single, stand-alone system must trace in some arcane manner the effect of better communication up and down the government corridor? Or do we simply try to estimate the beneficial effect that a system may have within the more circumscribed set of users who rely directly and with greater frequency on the information that will be stored and processed therein? The answer here boils down, again, to a question of measurement. Communication benefits are pervasive and will probably accrue to more indirect users—in many oblique ways—than we could ever imagine at the outset of a project (Hirschman 1967). Generally, it is difficult to predict the benefits of any program or project that exhibits great flexibility in responding to ad hoc user needs, and attempting to do so is a waste of time and effort. The consequence of focusing solely on a direct set of system beneficiaries is that total benefits will probably be underestimated. This is not really a disadvantage. If one is assured that a system can justify itself within more limited terms of reference, then total benefits are likely to be higher than anticipated. A good approach might be to formalize the participation of indirect beneficiaries; improved communication may add some useful arguments, even if their benefits cannot be directly measured and added to the calculus.

Once beneficiaries are identified, the more fundamental problem of measuring benefits becomes acute. For operations, the question may be a matter of measuring improved efficiency; the time saved in responding to a user request or in executing a task, the time that can be allocated to other more productive functions, and so on. Time, in operations, is of the essence, and so time becomes the essence of performance. Again, any additional benefit of a job better performed is essentially subjective, and the manager must use personal past experience and the opinions of trusted coworkers as subjective reality checks against the quantitative indicators initially collected. At management and policy levels, the tables are turned. Time is certainly a critical factor for many decisions taken here, but the degree to which time saved in accessing or analyzing information actually improves the quality of the decision itself cannot be quantified. Decisions are different here; they are more complex, are less routinized, and do not usually produce immediately definable consequences that can be directly attributed to the use of one or another critical datum. Therefore, benefits are much more likely to be measured subjectively, based on past experience and the persuasiveness of the manager serving the needs of policy debate.

In a situation where benefits promise to be substantial but measurement remains elusive, there is always the option of directing the analysis toward a relative comparison of costs. Cost effectiveness analysis is a scion of the larger family of benefit/cost techniques. It assumes that a package of well-defined services intrinsically has merit and, further, that these needs can be satisfied about equally well by each of several programmatic solutions. One then compares the alternative costs of providing one or more of the identified bundles of services.

Let us assume, for example, that a manager requires access to a land records file containing 5,000 records, on at least a daily basis, to produce summary reports and post changes on specific parcel records. Furthermore, she must also be able to produce detailed parcel information on an ad hoc basis many times during the day. One alternative might be to continue with a manual file system; another might be to use the excess capacity of the city's large mainframe system; and the last might be to purchase a stand-alone, desktop microcomputer system for the use of her clerk.

What is needed to establish the system? Data must be collected; a suitable file structure must be designed; data must be initially entered into the system; it must be further edited, or cleaned, then periodically updated; finally, both summary and detailed information must be available on a daily basis. It is not difficult to attach costs to each of these functions, according to some general yardstick such as entry cost per land record, both initially and over time. One would probably find, first, that the straw man of the analysis was the manual alternative, primarily because people costs comprise the largest expenditure in any system. Second, it is unlikely that the mainframe-based alternative would be as cost effective as the micro option because of the customized nature of the programming needed to accommodate a specific file structure; the opportunity costs of allocating machine time to functions that are regarded as less essential than payroll or accounting; and the technician time needed to install a remote terminal (in both the physical and the programming sense). Data capture and key entry times are likely to be comparable, but we are also assuming that the manager has not been forced to make any compromise in the quality of the service package required. Lest this example seem to imply a bias toward microcomputer-based solutions, one could perform the same analysis on the same problem but with the additional caveat that the manager be able to produce detailed parcel-level mapping to the tolerance that might be expected for legal or engineering work. In this case, a microcomputer-based alternative is likely to fall short of the goal.

One of the keys to successful system implementation, then, is to define, with as much detail as possible, the minimum package of benefits that direct end users find essential to their work, and the costs attached to each of several alternatives. With this accomplished, the system can be chosen and installed with some confidence that the decision was correct. More than just the application of benefit/cost technique is needed, though, to make the system work.

The Organization Revisited

Just as latent, unknown communication benefits are likely to emerge as systems start to mature, numerous unanticipated costs are also likely to mount in the initial stages of project implementation. Some of these are direct costs. Equipment may malfunction, software may crash, and data often are not available in a machine readable (or even humanly readable) form. These difficulties can sometimes become so acute that indirect costs, in the form of lost confidence, begin to cancel the very positive changes that the system could promote. Crises of confidence must be expected in any large undertaking, and when the project involves the integration of new, mysterious, and possibly threatening technologies, the option of rejecting change becomes tempting indeed, particularly in bureaucratic structures instinsically resistant to change. But bureaucratic procedures are shared by all large institutions, as are styles of leadership and management that implicitly encourage or discourage experimentation, risk-taking, and learning. Managers of successful computer system implementation programs employ explicit methods that embrace an innovative style (Peters and Waterman 1982).

The innovative style begins by rejecting the notion that all government workers wish to avoid responsibility, respond only to negative inducements, value security over change, and show little ambition. Some workers, of course, fit this description nicely, but a substantial number respond to challenge, seek new ideas, actively seek greater responsibility, and, most important, apply imagination and creativity to their daily tasks. It is workers of the latter type who must be identified and recruited to form the nucleus of an initial user group. They are the ones likely to benefit the most as well as to respond most ingeniously to the setbacks that will inevitably occur as systems are placed in operation.

Leadership must respond in kind with strong, visible evidence of support, even in the event of repeated setbacks, occasional mistakes, or modified ambitions. Such a response requires great faith, but leadership must be confident—and express its confidence—that important benefits will follow. Initial forays into end-user computing are best kept at a modest scale. They should be designed to produce as many tangible, immediate early results as possible.

Initial and continuing education not only is a great incentive to improved performance, but also increases the enthusiasm brought to the job. Enthusiasm is contagious, but it also can breed resentment on the part of others who missed the boat yet still hold crucial positions in the workstream. Further incentives will often work, but if not, the problem can often be removed with a transfer.

Scheduling time for reflection or an exchange of thought might seem to be a luxury in other kinds of work, but during implementation of a new system, regular user meetings are essential to coordinated efforts. Broadening the invitation list over time to include initially tangential but potentially more active users is a clever means of improving interdepartmental communication and increasing the system's cost effectiveness.

Finally, it is usually good to publicize the work. With politically sensitive issues, this might seem inadvisable, but there may be a tendency also to dismiss the victories that staff have won in improving the way their segment of government works. Although media coverage may seem to make a larger impact than other public relations ploys, a far more sustaining image may be cultivated by strengthening the bonds between government and community groups or voluntary organizations. Exchanging data with these groups is important; the strength of the system may be increased by opening up new channels of information.

This book contains only some of the answers needed to improve the choices that governments make every day. The various chapters have described a range of techniques that can be used with great, immediate effect to search for solutions to the many substantive issues facing local government today. In addition, the publications of the American Planning Association, the Urban and Regional Information Systems Association, the American Public Works Association, and many other organizations will also continue to make valuable contributions to the art and science of government. These works might not directly ameliorate the policy or professional identity crises that chronically preoccupy those who labor in the public sector, but they can certainly help planners find a stronger, more confident voice supported by a judicious mix of new technology and old-fashioned common sense.

References

Hirschman, Albert O. 1967. *Development Projects Observed.* Washington, D.C.: The Brookings Institution.

Peters, Thomas J., and Robert H. Waterman, Jr. 1982. *In Search of Excellence.* New York: Harper & Row.

Index

L

M

N

O

P

Z

About the Editors and Contributors

Editors

Mathew E. MacIver is a developer and planning consultant based in Boston. He has directed development projects in Africa and the United States. As educational coordinator at the Lincoln Institute of Land Policy, he conducted research and courses in computer-assisted property appraisal and geographic information systems.

Jan Schreiber, Ph.D., is a research scientist and consultant. At the Lincoln Institute of Land Policy, he was project director of the Cleveland LMS project during its final year. A social scientist with extensive microcomputer experience, he has served as senior analyst at several major research organizations and as president of the Social Science Research Institute.

Contributors

John R. Fauquier, Ph.D., has worked as a city planner and project manager with the city of Cleveland, Ohio. He is currently a planning consultant with the Toronto firm of Woods Gordon.

Rolf Goetze, Ph.D., served as director of housing revitalization for the Boston Redevelopment Authority. The author of several books on housing and neighborhood change, he is a consultant in housing and neighborhood development policy.

Alven H. S. Lam, formerly senior planner with the Teipei (Taiwan) municipal government, is now systems analyst and planner at the Lincoln Institute of Land Policy, where he conducts applications research in geographic information systems.

Neil G. Sipe, formerly with the Bureau of Economic and Business Research, University of Florida, is currently an analyst with M.G. Lewis Econometrics of Orlando. He has written extensively about microcomputer applications and growth management issues in local government.